my

~~awesome~~ ~~beautiful~~

badass

book of saints

"Maria Morera Johnson's *My Badass Book of Saints* delivers a heavy-weight message of holiness with the lightest of touches and somehow manages a knockout punch. Her entertaining list of modern women of faith and their saintly counterparts exhorts women toward sainthood and says, 'Yes, this can be you, too, if you want it.' It's the wanting, after all—the pursuit of sainthood despite obstacles malicious or well-meant—that brings out the badass, fearless trust that hones a saint."

Elizabeth Scalia
Catholic blogger and author of *Strange Gods*

"In pages riddled with humor and gripping stories, I was shocked to realize that I shared qualities with great women I always thought were out of my league. In the lives of these ordinary, sometimes feisty women I found my story, and as many of them are now saints, I found an incredible conviction to live my ordinary life loving God and allowing him to do extraordinary things through me . . . with a little help from my new friends!"

Kelly Wahlquist
Founder of Women In the New Evangelization
Author of *Created to Relate*

"This is a book that's not afraid to talk of the beautiful mess, where faith meets real life, where saints and mortals coexist, one cheering the other on to glory."

Pat Gohn
Author of *Blessed, Beautiful, and Bodacious*

"Maria Johnson is a badass. As she shares herself in these pages, her stories—and those of these courageous women—inspire us to believe that our own sometimes seemingly ordinary lives and what we do with them can be enough. For ourselves and for God."

Shelly Henley Kelly and Lisa Henley Jones
Catholic bloggers and contributors to *CatholicMom.com*

"In a world where heroism has become synonymous with superheroes, Maria Morera Johnson argues for a scandalous interpretation. Real heroism, the kind that adds up to 'true greatness,' she says, is about our day by day offering of all that is 'boring and hard and unpalatable' in the quotidian moments of our life. To give us courage to become extra-ordinary in this ordinary journey, Johnson provides us as models a notable communion of women—some recognized officially as saints by the Church and others simply holy women, all of whom made a deliberate choice to stand on the strength of their convictions. As a Cuban immigrant and refugee, Johnson knows intimately the cost of this faith quest. With reflective and insightful understanding, she weaves together her own life story and that of women who have enabled her to stand strong and faithful in her Catholic faith. They impacted her life. They will impact yours, too!"

María de Lourdes Ruiz Scaperlanda
Catholic blogger and writer

"Maria Johnson is brave, boisterous, loving, and real. Having worked firsthand with her on several writing projects, we can honestly say we've been excitedly awaiting this inaugural and masterful book for more than a decade."

Greg and Jennifer Willits
Hosts of *The Catholics Next Door*

"We often look at the great saints of the Church and know few details about them apart from the way they met their end. To know the passionate commitment to faith that strengthened them to make those final sacrifices? More of that, please."

Matt Swaim
Host of the *Son Rise Morning Show*

"Each of us has an opportunity to be a beacon of hope to those around us. Thank you, Maria, for writing and sharing this remarkable collection of courage and inspiration."

Immaculée Ilibagiza
Rwandan holocaust survivor and author of *Left to Tell*

My ~~awesome~~ ~~beautiful~~ badass book of saints

Courageous
Women
Who Showed
Me How
to Live

MARIA MORERA JOHNSON

AVE MARIA PRESS AVE Notre Dame, Indiana

© 2015 by Maria Morera Johnson

Foreword © 2015 by Pat Gohn

All rights reserved. No part of this book may be used or reproduced in any manner whatsoever, except in the case of reprints in the context of reviews, without written permission from Ave Maria Press®, Inc., P.O. Box 428, Notre Dame, IN 46556, 1-800-282-1865.

Founded in 1865, Ave Maria Press is a ministry of the United States Province of Holy Cross.

www.avemariapress.com

Paperback: ISBN-13 978-1-59471-632-4

E-book: ISBN-13 978-1-59471-633-1

Cover image © Thinkstock.com.

Cover and text design by Katherine Robinson.

Printed and bound in the United States of America.

Library of Congress Cataloging-in-Publication Data
Johnson, Maria Morera.
  My badass book of saints : courageous women who showed me how to live / Maria Morera Johnson.
    pages cm
  Includes bibliographical references.
  ISBN 978-1-59471-632-4 -- ISBN 1-59471-632-3
  1. Christian women saints--Biography. 2. Christian women--Biography. I. Title.
  BX4656.J64 2015
  282.092'52--dc23
  [B]
                    2015025734

For Mami,
who first put a pencil
in my hand
to write my first words,

and Pop,
who always read them and asked for more.

~~~~~~

Maybe this book ought to have a black leather jacket. *Butler's Lives of the Saints* it ain't.

With all due respect to that historian's renowned and venerable collection, *Butler's Lives of the Saints* reads like an encyclopedia: dates and facts ordered in a neat and traditional catalog.

In truth, there is nothing neat and orderly about saint making *at all*. The Spirit blows where it wills. Indeed, the Lord does not call those who are worthy but those he wills to call. The thing about saints is that they start out with the same raw materials we all have and in the same beautiful mess we are all in.

All saints in heaven were sinners on earth. They just figured out where to find grace and how to live by it. Knowing God changed them in ways known only to them, but lucky for us, we can see the good—the holy influence—they left behind.

Saints wore skin just as we do. Moreover, they had skin in the game in the cosmic duel between good and evil. Venturing into *Butler's* we discover saints with pasts, some with outlandish or formidable histories. Some were so tough they were not to be messed with. Some were troublemakers who—whether from grace, or their own experience, or a combination of both—knew how to handle trouble.

Be honest: Is that the way we envision *women* saints? Read on.

Maria Morera Johnson, a college professor with degrees in literature and education, is a self-declared fan of the sci-fi and superhero genres. She knows how to tell a good story, yet *My Badass Book of Saints: Courageous Women Who Showed Me How to Live* proves she knows truth from fiction. Her stories describe real-life women who faced down outlaws in the Old West, genocide in Rwanda, convicts in a Tijuana prison, and oppressive regimes in Europe and Cuba. Maria also chronicles canonized saints, both well-known and obscure. Their strength, verve, and feminine genius may raise an eyebrow or two, but their powerful witness will inspire women seeking ways to live out a strong and uncompromising faith in a dangerous world.

Maria's keen and unpretentious storytelling offers insights from her own soul for women who yearn for more. She opens up for us her inner dialogue with a cadre of impressive (and sometimes impish) saints. Plus, she profiles dynamic women who made history, and even shares personal stories about women close to her. Maria recounts how God used these women to breathe new life into her once-sagging faith through their heroism, fortitude, friendship, intercession, and—well, let's just say it—their *badass* way of overcoming adversities, dealing with sin without crushing the human spirit, and serving God by doing the seemingly impossible under pitiable circumstances. Their undaunted chutzpah captures our attention.

Who are the saints and would-be saints who accompany us in our lives? Some of us might be named after a saint; Maria introduces us to her namesake in the concluding chapter. Others might look to a relative, friend, or mentor whose encouragement and influence has been pivotal or life changing. This book reminds us that we are not alone in life—the saints in heaven accompany us! And a host of convincing role models can be found on earth, too.

St. Augustine is often credited with the idea that "there is no saint without a past, no sinner without a future."

So, what about *us*? Do we dare imagine ourselves, maybe in our wildest dreams, becoming saints?

The only mental images of saints we have may be white plaster statues in churches or paintings and icons from long ago. Rather than perceive the holy boldness they possessed, we falsely picture their lives shrouded in an unrealistic piety or an unreachable cleanliness-that's-next-to-godliness. It's sometimes hard to imagine them as *real*. Or messy. Or messed up. Or messin' with people.

That's what I like about this book. It introduces saints who smash the holier-than-thou and goody-two-shoes boxes we sometimes shut them in.

Nobody's dissing piety or faithfulness here. There are no saints without these qualities. But women of holy influence come in a variety of shapes and sizes, temperaments and tempers. And they come to their faith in God through countless circumstances and circuitous channels.

God beckons to us through a variety of voices . . . some offbeat and some in tune. Who inspires me is likely different from who might inspire you. Maria's litany of the courageous "whos" in her life is infectious: she shows us the value of getting to know a saint or two who might be more like us than we'd care to admit, or one who might shock us into a new and more courageous way of living. This is a book that's not afraid to wade into the beautiful mess where faith meets real life—where saints and mortals coexist, cheering each other on to glory.

In the first chapter, Maria writes:

> The path to sainthood starts—and ends—with my desire to act for the love of God. I think I can do that. . . . It'll just take a little audacity on my part . . . to banish the silly notion that "they don't make women like that anymore."

God is indeed still in the business of creating women who are destined to do great things. And I think God loves it when women find ways to work together for the greater good.

Since I do a lot of writing for Catholic organizations, I take note of writers who get my attention. I first "met" Maria Johnson in 2007 when her name scrolled by in the writing credits for *That Catholic Show*, a quirky and fun YouTube video series created by Greg and Jennifer Willits of Rosary Army.

Maria and I met in person at a conference a year later in Atlanta, close to her home. Our friendship grew during months of collaboration to bring the 2010 version of that same conference—SQPN's Catholic New Media Conference—to Boston, near where I live.

We discovered that we constituted a mutual admiration society. Not only was I a fan of the podcasts Maria collaborated on in her off-hours from teaching, but *she* had been reading all *my* columns and blog posts for years. Phone chats and social media conversations became common. We share a love for family, our faith, countless books and articles, and all things beach.

Both of us travel periodically for speaking engagements. There have been an uncanny number of instances when my work has brought me to or through Georgia and Maria's has sent her to New England. When we do see each other, it's a true celebration with wine, good food, chocolate, and coffee. Lots of coffee.

We read (and sometimes edit) each other's work and pray for each other. And God has opened doors for us to work together on a few creative endeavors. It's a gift to be able to contribute, in this small way, to Maria's book of saints.

So, inquiring minds want to know: Is Maria Morera Johnson a *badass*?

Let me put it this way: As a Scrabble opponent, she is formidable. As a teacher, she's won top awards in her field. As a writer, she's self-effacing and nuanced, even in her second language. As a friend, she has your back and fights the good fight of faithful friendship (translation: there's more than one bead in your honor on her rosary).

Speaking of translations, my bilingual pal Maria Begoña was an early reader of a book I wrote for women—*Blessed, Beautiful, and Bodacious*. When I asked how her Spanish-speaking loved ones were faring reading my book, she told me that the word *bodacious* does not translate well into Spanish. She explained that it is rendered more as *badass*.

Oh.

"Well then," I told her, "that's the book you'll have to write, *amiga.*"

God doesn't miss a thing—and he has a sense of humor.

Next time Maria comes to Boston, I'm totally taking her shopping for a black leather jacket.

Pat Gohn
Author of *Blessed, Beautiful, and Bodacious*

~~~~~~

from badass to blessed

Surrounding Myself with Extraordinary Women Who Inspire Me

~~~~~~

If you run your finger along the back of my left ear, you can feel the raised scar from the time I nearly lopped off my ear when I was a little girl.

It happened quickly. I tied my bath towel around my neck to make a Superman cape and secured it with a wooden clothespin (the kind with the spring) before bravely climbing up my desk and onto the top of my dresser.

From there I could survey my whole room. I figured if I leaped straight out I could fly for a couple of seconds before landing safely on my bed. With a deep breath, I sprang. It was a spectacular launch, an amazing flight . . . followed by a loud thump when I missed my bed and grazed the corner of the night table with my head.

I don't know which alerted my parents—the house shaking or my screams. Everything after that was a blur until I found myself lying on my back in an operating room staring at the cold surgical light. I could hear the sound of the thread being pulled through my ear as the doctor sewed up the damage.

You'd think I'd have learned something from this little adventure. Oh, I don't know, perhaps the important lesson that little girls can't fly? I didn't. Within months I was sporting a four-inch scar down the length of my cheek, from eye to chin, from a second failed attempt at flight—this time I'd jumped out of a tree, trying to swing like Tarzan. I didn't understand the physics of it: a static branch looked as though it could swing like a jungle vine. Maybe.

I was lucky to have avoided breaking bones, not to mention losing my eye. These failures never deterred me, and if I'm being totally honest, I'll confess that part of me is still ready to parachute out of an airplane. I just need somebody to dare me.

La Tremenda

My long-suffering mother knows this about me. She calls me *tremenda*, a Spanish word that has many layers of meaning. To look at it, you might think it translates handily as *tremendous*, but that's not quite right. It does mean tremendous, sometimes. It also means terrific, and terrible. It translates as bold. Daring. Fearless. Stalwart. Smart. Courageous. In a lot of cases, it can be used as a modifier to express both judge-y disdain and profound admiration.

But mostly it means *badass*.

The sensibilities for the word are a little looser in Spanish, but as a lover of words, I can't help but be drawn to the nuances inherent in using a word that carries a little shock value.

Sometimes we need a little shock in our lives to get our attention. Not too much, though. Vulgarity for its own sake precludes the rich opportunity for communication opened up by an unexpected zinger such as *badass*. It gets your attention, and believe me, the women in these pages deserve our attention. They certainly got mine.

As a young woman, I suffered under the misconception that to pursue a life of holiness meant to lead a boring life filled with long periods of contemplation and silence. I longed to find role models who matched my own approach to life—saints with boisterous laughs and quick tongues that sometimes got them in trouble, women unafraid to be themselves and say what was on their minds, even if they ruffled a few feathers.

In short, I longed to discover badass women who lived lives of real holiness. Women with whom, perhaps, I might have a little in common.

As a girl, I loved excitement. I loved adventure. (I still do.) Those adventures always seemed to be a good idea—too many times to the dismay of my poor mother, who probably owned stock in Mercurochrome. Evidently I had to survive Mercurochrome poisoning to make it to adulthood.

Besides the aerial adventures, there was nothing extraordinary about my childhood. It was an idyllic time. We lived in a complex of townhouse apartments. We knew all our neighbors. Our mothers stayed home and took care of us. Our fathers went to work, some in the mornings to factories, others, like my father, in the early evening to work in the restaurants and nightclubs of downtown Atlanta.

I didn't know we lived in an immigrant ghetto populated suddenly by an influx of Cuban refugees. I just knew I spoke like everybody else, except for my next-door neighbor Elizabeth, who spoke a different way. In no time, I could speak like her and a couple of the other kids from down the street, but I had no word for *bilingual*. And the concept of growing up bicultural wasn't a notion even in the minds of the adults.

I knew that I was loved, that I had friends, and that I had to be home before the streetlights came on. It was, to me, a fairy-tale childhood.

Some of my earliest memories are of being happy in a little *barrio* in the Deep South in the middle of the civil rights movement. But that's not where the story began.

Our family's chapter began with my father's grit and desire to forge a new life for his young family, away from the dangers of a communist regime. And yet the rest of the story, as Paul Harvey used to say, is my mother's.

My Badass Family

My mother is the most badass woman I know. Apparently, she gets it from *her* mother. I was a teenager before I could begin to appreciate what these women had gone through. I was a wife, and then a young mother, before I began to understand the inner resources they must have possessed to survive.

These remarkable women, my mother and grandmother, both left behind their families, their homes, everything they had ever known, in the pursuit of freedom so that one day I could grow up free to practice my religion and pursue my dreams. They wanted me to have the freedom that had been denied to them.

My mother really never spoke of this sacrifice. She was busy working around the house doing the same things other moms did. She cooked. She cleaned. She sewed. She nurtured me and my brother and sister.

I took her for granted in the comfortable way so many children do. I didn't want for anything, so I didn't know there must have been hard times and struggles. We eventually moved out of the townhouse and into a house in the suburbs—and our friends from those early days followed us. We were living the American Dream, and I was going to school and becoming an obnoxious teenager.

Lucky for me, we all survived those turbulent years, and I came out of it for the better. Soon, I was pursuing my own dreams. I married right out of college and was swept away to live in Germany for a few years when my husband was in the army. My mother might have made a passing comment about my going full circle and returning to Europe, but I blew it off, still not ready to understand her story. *My* story, too.

You see, my mother and her mother before her fled oppressive political regimes. My grandmother and grandfather left Spain during World War II, Basque nationals running from an oppressive government and the bombings of Basque villages. I remember staring at Picasso's *Guernica* at the Museum of Modern Art in New York in the 1970s and thinking, *That is my story*. My mother's parents emigrated to Cuba.

Then, in 1962, just months before the Cuban Missile Crisis, my father journeyed to America to find a job and an apartment, leaving my mother, pregnant with me, behind in Cuba. He never imagined that the October Crisis would precipitate a forced separation that lasted years. My mother would not be reunited with my father until 1966—when we were able to make it to the United States and I finally *met* my father.

Decades later, after I had started my own family, I discovered a box of photographs and mementos that my parents were putting into picture albums. I held and read the telegram announcing my birth that my grandfather sent from Cuba to my father in the United States. I then read my father's response, addressed to me, telling me how much he loved me and yearned to meet me soon.

I was undone by those little slips of paper, weeping big, fat, hot tears for my mother, for my father, for me. As a young parent, I couldn't fathom what it would be like to be separated from my child. I couldn't imagine losing my husband to a political machine, never knowing whether we would be reunited. It was too much for me in the moment; even now, twenty-five or more years removed from that discovery, the memory of intense heat from those tears still shocks me.

I recognized, finally, that the past doesn't go away: it lays a foundation for the future. Although I've never made a conscious effort to work with immigrant populations and the marginalization many of them experience in society, I've realized quite recently that I do find ways to put a balm on the pain of those immigrants I encounter.

Finding My Purpose

One of the things I appreciate about midlife is the ability to reflect. I often look back on my life in astonishment, able in retrospect to see where God's hand has written entire sections to prepare me for things to come. It's a gift for which I'm thankful because it brings me a great deal of consolation.

I need consolation because I'm still that resistant child with the independent spirit. I fly off dressers and jump out of trees and don't look before I leap. Just as I said no to my parents when they wanted me to stay out of trees, I've repeatedly said no to the Holy Spirit and his plan for me. Sometimes quite loudly. It has resulted in some bumps and bruises along the way, but it has also taken me on some unusual adventures.

When I refused, flat out, to become a teacher in spite of some serious recruitment on the part of an excellent educator who saw the spark of potential in me, I became instead a "corporate trainer teaching employability skills" to Cuban and Haitian immigrants in Little Havana, Miami.

That's a fancy name for teacher, isn't it?

When I was a newlywed living in Europe while my husband served in the army, the only job available was substitute teacher. The principal liked me so much he made me a permanent kindergarten sub. I thought I was going to have a nervous breakdown so I applied for a job as a technical writer.

I wanted to be a writer. I got the job. What did I do all day? I created PowerPoint presentations for a directorate in the Department of Defense. In short, I wrote curriculum.

My husband finished his enlistment, and we returned to Miami, where he pursued a career in computer science and I got back my old job as a trainer. Right up until I became pregnant and needed some health insurance. What saved me? The signing bonus and benefits package . . . from my job as an English teacher in the very high school that graduated me.

I taught remedial English to a rough crowd of gangsters, a group of kids who believed everyone in the system had given up on them. I lived my own episodes of *Welcome Back, Kotter* (a sitcom from the seventies in which a former student returns to an inner-city school as the teacher).

Within a few years my husband pursued new opportunities in Georgia, and the family relocated. I quit teaching and returned to technical writing—it was the happiest day of my adult working life. I became a bilingual freelancer, and within months I was translating documents for the local schools. A short time later, the county mental health division hired me to teach the writing and journaling portion of a women's therapy group. That was the first time I could clearly discern what God was doing: all my experiences up to that point had prepared me to provide not just instruction in composition, but the compassion and empathy needed to help the women write the stories hidden in their hearts.

Everybody has a story. Some are broken by it and don't know how to write new and better chapters. Others celebrate it. I've been drawn to life stories ever since I taught that class.

Holy Cards, Holy Women, *Holy Smoke!*

These pages are filled with the life stories of some extraordinary women—women who fought against the elements, fought against enemies both foreign and domestic, fought against society. Injustice. Inequality. *The odds.*

Some of these women are saints. Some of them are saints in the making. And still others ought to be named saints. The common denominator among them is the amazing way they rose out of their ordinary circumstances to commit acts of audacity: bold, daring, plucky, fearless acts.

I knew many of these women from holy cards or other Church pamphlets, but for the most part they remained one-dimensional. Their indomitable spirits were reduced to three or four talking points in a sidebar and, if they are saints, maybe a quick reference list of their patronage. Who were they, really? And why would I want to emulate them?

The short answer is that I want to surround myself with extraordinary women. There was a time when I would have been content with fictional heroines in stories or superheroes in comic books. The little girl who jumped off dressers would have loved to be friends with Wonder Woman and have adventures with the Justice League. I focused on extraordinary feats of daring to escape the drudgery of the ordinary, missing the importance of these little daily tasks.

The years of separation from extended family robbed me of strong role models within the family, but I was blessed without realizing it by my mother's friends, women who formed a strong spiritual bond in community. Like those imaginary superheroes and my mother's real circle of friends, the amazing women in these pages accomplished the extraordinary because it was the right thing to do.

Now in midlife, I find myself picking up my old holy cards and looking past the dull pictures and facts to see the real women who are my spiritual role models. Their holy lives inspire me to live my life in fulfillment of my baptismal promises . . . and yet I also love that these women tend to be *tremenda*, a little badass, too.

I knew many of these saints from primers in elementary school: St. Teresa of Avila, St. Joan of Arc, and St. Catherine of Siena. Some of the other saints were new to me, if not by name then certainly because of their unique stories. A few of them, such as St. Gianna Beretta Molla and St. Rita of Cascia, have quickly become my go-to saints.

I look to these saints so I can imitate them and grow in their virtues, but also so I can call upon them for prayer. They are powerful intercessors. I hope you also find inspiration in the women I feature in these pages. They have become a part of my extended family, my sisters in Christ. And like the good sisters they are, they all point to our ultimate spiritual model: the Blessed Virgin Mary.

How to Use This Book

My Badass Book of Saints contains both questions to ponder at the end of each chapter and group discussion questions designed for a six-week study at the end of the book. Explore the works listed in the resources section at the back of the book to learn more about these inspiring women.

questions to ponder

1. Think about the title of the book. Do you find it shocking, or does a part of you smirk a little and wonder about the content? How do you think this book will compare to other books on the saints you've already read?

2. What does the author say about her choice to use the word *badass*?

3. The author uses the Spanish word *tremenda*. Define it. Are you *tremenda*?

~~~~~~

audacious sisters who acted fearlessly

Sr. Blandina Segale and St. Teresa of Avila

~~~~~~

Entertain acts of audacity.

~Dr. Curtis Johnson, educator

I have a soft spot in my heart for nuns toting guns.

Some years ago, I walked into a friend's office while she was putting up a new calendar. The calendar featured pictures of nuns doing all the ordinary things regular people do. Because, you know, nuns are regular people. They just have a habit of dressing differently.

My friend and I giggled happily as we went through all the months in the calendar, marveling at the fun pictures: nuns playing Skee-Ball on a boardwalk, nuns on bicycles. Bowling nuns. And then we saw the badass sisters: nuns holding guns.

There they were, lined up in their habits, wielding rifles like pros. Clearly nobody was going to get past *them* without encountering the business end of those guns. We laughed and laughed at this wild image. But it probably wasn't that unusual. Missionary religious sisters and nuns have traveled to all kinds of isolated destinations. Maybe they were really good hunters.

Right.

I forgot about that calendar until recently, when I noticed a headline in *The Huffington Post* calling Sr. Blandina Segale of the Sisters of Charity the "Fastest Nun in the West." The headline not only captured my heart, but it tickled my love of wordplay and a good pun. Fastest nun, eh? I had to read more. The article spoke about her newly opened cause for canonization, but the link bait worked—I was drawn to images of a showdown on Main Street in the middle of a deserted town. I wasn't too far from the truth.

A Fearless Trailblazer

Like so many of the other religious sisters settling in the United States throughout the nineteenth and early twentieth centuries, Sr. Blandina started off with a vocation to serve God, never imagining it would lead her to the Wild West.

The beginning of Maria Rosa Segale's story is not extraordinary. She was born in Italy in 1850 and immigrated to the United States, settling with her family in Ohio. As a young girl, she told her family that she wanted to join the Sisters of Charity, and when she turned sixteen she entered the novitiate, taking the name Blandina. She went to teach in the Cincinnati and Dayton areas.

This is when the story twists. One day, Sr. Blandina heard she would be transferred to Trinidad. She thought she was going to Trinidad in the *West Indies* and got excited about this new adventure. (I can't blame her.) Unfortunately, she learned soon enough that she wasn't going to the West Indies, but rather to the American West . . . to Trinidad, *Colorado.*

Trinidad, Colorado, was no Caribbean paradise. When she arrived Sr. Blandina encountered a violent town filled with hardship and lawlessness. The residents often took justice into their own hands, forming lynch mobs to handle dangerous outlaws.

Now, one would not think that a twenty-two-year-old religious sister would have much influence in such an environment. But Sr. Blandina managed to do the unthinkable, as commemorated in the CBS series *Death Valley Days*: she squelched one of those lynch mobs by bringing the accused to the bedside of the dying man he had assaulted. The dying man, through Sr. Blandina's intercession, forgave his aggressor. As a result, the accused man was tried in a court of law rather than by a vigilante mob in the streets.

I love that! What could inspire a young woman to face a mob intent on hanging a man? She stood on the strength of her convictions. She knew that a violent response to violence generally leads to more violence. Regardless of whether the accused man was found guilty in his trial, Sr. Blandina's intervention accomplished a great deal: She stopped an angry mob from behaving vindictively, saving those men from the inhumane desire to repay one heinous act with another one. She helped a grievously wounded man face his own death and judgment by forgiving the man who caused it. And by encouraging the accused man to face his victim and seek forgiveness, she may have stirred something in his heart as well.

To that crowd, Sr. Blandina's audacious witness to Christ's mercy was as remarkable as it seems to us today. For Sr. Blandina, it was just another day. After all, she faced Billy the Kid not once, but three times in her life! Perhaps she had grown so accustomed to the unsavory aspects of life in this Western town that she became immune to the rough element. Or, what is more likely, she saw beyond the baseness of the human condition and recognized the opportunity to save souls.

Because of her dedication to upholding the human dignity of every person, even Billy the Kid gave her a well-deserved measure of respect that saved her life, and likely those of others as well. Their first meeting occurred when one of the men in Billy's gang was severely wounded and rejected by the local doctors because of his criminal behavior. Sr. Blandina took in the ailing man and tended his gunshot wound. When Billy the Kid arrived, intent on killing the doctors who had denied one of his men medical treatment, the spunky Sr. Blandina convinced him to let the doctors live. Just imagine Sr. Blandina standing up to her full petite height and sternly telling, *telling*, a hardened criminal to back down. *Or else.*

This would not be her last encounter with the outlaw. She met Billy the Kid again when his gang overran a wagon train she was traveling in. But when Billy the Kid looked inside Sr. Blandina's wagon and recognized her, he tipped his hat in salutation and left the group unharmed.

Her third and final encounter with Billy the Kid demonstrates something of her compassion for all people, especially those she cared for—regardless of their station in life or reputation. While visiting a man in jail, she once again found herself face-to-face with Billy the Kid; this time he was in one of the cells. She recalled that Billy the Kid spoke in defense of the man she went to visit, revealing some of his own regrets in the process. Sister observed that Billy the Kid might have lived a better life had he chosen the right path instead of the wrong path. She didn't judge him harshly, but merely observed that his choices led him to that place in his life.

Isn't that true for all of us?

Brave Nuns in the Wilderness

It's easy to imagine that the pragmatic Sr. Blandina approached her daily duties with the same kind of understated heroism, focused not on recounting tales of high adventure in the midst of outlaws in the Wild West, but on building schools and hospitals in Trinidad, Colorado (and later Santa Fe, New Mexico). Her work with Native Americans and Mexicans, in particular, makes her a saint for today.

Her entire life was an act of audacity that began at her birth, when her mother, Giovanna, took the infant Maria Rosa to the church at Monteallegro in Italy and presented her to the Blessed Virgin Mary, praying for her daughter "to help mankind, *Madre*

Mia, to comfort the sorrowful . . . to harbor the harborless . . . to visit the sick . . . to teach your ways to mankind" (Segale 2).

Sr. Blandina grew up to do all those things, and more. She founded public schools, Catholic schools, orphanages, and hospitals in Colorado and then in New Mexico—including St. Joseph's Hospital in Albuquerque—before returning to Cincinnati, where she founded The Santa Maria Institute to serve Italian immigrants to the area. That organization continues today as Santa Maria Community Services.

Although she continues to make headlines because of her audacious behavior around hardened criminals, Sr. Blandina's most heroic accomplishment is her lifetime of diligence and daily sacrifice in the face of poverty and hardship.

The image of gun-toting nuns, while funny to my modern sensibilities, no doubt reveals something significant about what it took to be a woman settling in the American West. These women needed spirit and a large measure of courage just to survive. After all, they were facing much more than just a hostile environment.

Missionary nuns were settling throughout the western part of the country even before the days of rough cowboys and cattlemen. Sometimes they accompanied missionary priests, but often they worked alone. These sisters helped to build the American West. To say these women were brave doesn't seem enough. They had the stamina and drive to follow through with their mission, whether that mission was administrative support of an existing community or founding new communities, schools, and hospitals.

There was nothing romantic in this work. It wasn't just perilous; it must have been boring and tedious at times, too. Still, my imagination runs wild considering the more unsavory experiences these women must have encountered. After all, violent conflict filled those days with the kind of lawlessness that physically endangered women.

My wilderness is filled not with gunmen and washed out trails, but with twenty-first-century psychological equivalents: Too much structured time. Too many electronic distractions.

Feelings of isolation and loneliness due to distance from loved ones.

But Sr. Blandina and others like her must have faced down such familiar unseen perils as hopelessness, insecurity, and fear along with the visible dangers. These roadblocks to audacious living strike me when I least expect it. Sometimes the to-do lists at home and work become so overwhelming that I despair of ever finishing. I lose confidence in my ability to complete the tasks before me. And I'm surprised to discover that I am just as likely to fear success as I am failure. Yet I strive to follow the example set before me by these strong pioneering women.

A Mystical Reformer

Saints' histories, too, are filled with stories of women whose *yes* to God required them to face unimaginable hardship in order to do God's will and, as Sr. Blandina's mother Giovanna prayed, "to teach [his] ways to mankind."

Centuries before Sr. Blandina and others like her went into unknown mission fields and built communities, St. Teresa of Avila, a Carmelite nun, did the same, founding numerous convents and monasteries across Spain and parts of Portugal after leading a reform of the Carmelite Order.

If ever there was a saint who deserved my apologies, it would be dear St. Teresa. My family has long had a devotion to her. In fact, my mother and her sisters and my mother-in-law and *her* sisters all attended a school in Cuba named after St. Teresa of Avila and run by Carmelite nuns. Had political and religious oppression not caused the closing of the school and convent, I, too, would have been a graduate of that esteemed school. As it happens, I was brought to the United States as an immigrant and was educated by a different order of religious sisters, the Grey Nuns of the Sacred Heart. Nevertheless, St. Teresa was a constant presence in my life as I was growing up, if not overtly, then definitely in the subtle ways in which my mother's faith had been formed and, in turn, how she formed my faith.

I can say this—I met the yearly St. Teresa School reunions with my mother's classmates and former teachers, aging nuns who all wanted to meet me, with the disdain only a teenage girl could muster. I rolled my eyes, huffed and puffed about all the places I *could* be instead of there, but nevertheless endured Masses and endless Rosaries and Holy Hours at these meetings. The ever-present statue of St. Teresa seemed to stare sternly at me during the receptions. Little did I know that decades later I would choose the very same St. Teresa of Avila as my patron saint.

The St. Teresa I had known while growing up was an impos-ing woman. When I was just a girl, Pope Paul VI declared her a Doctor of the Church, and ever after I thought of her as a dour old saint, serious and severe, having nothing at all in common with me. In my child's mind, St. Teresa was not only holy—something I would never be—but also impossible to emulate. It turns out I had much more in common with St. Teresa than I could ever imagine.

A couple of years ago while recording an episode of *Cath-olic Weekend*, a weekly panel talk show I cohost, I expressed my regret at never having chosen a confirmation saint. Escalating tensions during the communist revolution in Cuba caused a shortage of priests, making prevalent the practice of infant con-firmation. Confirmed before I knew anything about the faith, I wasn't able to choose a saint for myself.

When it finally occurred to me, through that *Catholic Week-end* taping, that I could simply choose a patron saint, I spent the next year reading about various saints before discovering what I should have known all along: St. Teresa of Avila, Doctor of the Church, reformer of religious orders, was a formidable woman. Her strength of character and resolve were such that she could probably run multinational corporations today. She founded seventeen convents and fifteen friaries after the age of fifty, and all this despite opposition from within her order, from the clergy in her community, and from residents in the villages where she established new cloisters.

St. Teresa faced many of the same trials that Sr. Blandina and her counterparts faced when traveling across hostile lands. To found the new convents and monasteries, she traveled by mule or carriage all over Spain and suffered the indignities of the road. Poor weather, heat, cold, starvation—these were real dangers, not to mention the threat of attack in hostile areas.

I had always assumed that St. Teresa traveled in large caravans with protective entourages. After all, she was establishing convents—surely she would bring supplies and people. As it turns out, that wasn't always the case. In fact, hardship was the common denominator in her labors. One story in particular stands out as an example of the hardships she endured, not to mention her pragmatic resiliency. When founding the convent in Salamanca, St. Teresa brought only one nun with her as a companion. They established the convent in an existing house, but it had no amenities. There was no furniture. It was dirty and in disrepair. When evening came and it was time to retire, they had only straw for beds.

St. Teresa found comfort in the straw—she often made sure to bring straw for this very purpose—but her companion was quite desolate. Teresa inquired about the nun's nervousness and was startled by the woman's response: she asked how St. Teresa would handle the corpse if the nun were to die that night.

Taken aback by such a thought, St. Teresa told the companion to go to sleep, that she'd worry about it only if she needed to. When I first read this, I thought it was hilarious. The whole exchange sounds a little surreal, but the more I consider it, the more I realize that St. Teresa must have had such thoughts herself. The hardship, danger, and desolation were real. Yet in all of it, St. Teresa stood strong in her convictions, most of all in her love of the Lord Jesus Christ, which helped her surmount all the trials she faced.

Of course, I read two of her important works on spirituality, *The Interior Castle* and *The Way of Perfection*. I admit this kind of reading was new to me; I needed a bit of hand-holding to get through it. I had more questions than answers, but I didn't give up, reading more and more of her writing. Her spiritual life, and the mystical experiences she describes, seemed far beyond what I could possibly achieve.

It was difficult to grasp the meaning of her mystical experiences. Having seen Bernini's famous sculpture depicting her ecstasy, I was familiar with her spiritual espousal to Christ and the "transverberation" of her heart, the piercing dart and great joy she experienced while deep in prayer that caused her to long for the day when she would die and be united with Christ in heaven. Her ability to levitate during prayer was also something far beyond my understanding.

A Woman Like Me

And yet St. Teresa had other qualities I read about and could relate to. She suffered from a number of ailments, including headaches. I suffer from migraines. She wrote poems and prayerful verses on scraps of paper. So do I.

She entered the convent without a strong vocation. I began my career as an educator in the same way—it just seemed like the thing to do. She didn't experience a deep conversion until later in life. I can relate to that, too.

She had a wicked sense of humor. I see the funny side of things. A humorous outlook is something I admire a great deal; I think we can use humor to deflate tensions in confrontations or put someone at ease, especially if there is some awkwardness present in the exchange. A quick wit can find humor in a situation and make that the focus while stating a correction that carries weight—a correction that nips but doesn't bite.

One of my favorite stories about her quick wit also reveals a little bit of St. Teresa's charm. It seems that a male visitor to the convent had the effrontery to comment on her pretty bare feet. That situation had to have been mortifying for her—not just the man's boldness in speech, but the personal violation. Instead of shying away and hiding, St. Teresa boldly suggested he get a good look because it would be the last time he would have that opportunity. Her meaning, of course, was that he was no longer welcome at the convent. I suspect he understood.

Images of St. Teresa often depict her carrying a statue of the Infant Jesus, which I think is a little weird. Of course, I work with

a bobblehead of Mother Teresa of Calcutta on my desk. I guess
we get our inspiration where we can.

And then I discovered this quote of hers: "May God protect
me from gloomy saints." I laughed, realizing that she might
cringe to know I perceived *her* as a gloomy saint. That statement—a prayer, really, for deliverance—changed everything for
me. With that simple quote, St. Teresa became human for me.

She was a woman, like me. And therefore I, as a woman,
could be like her.

Ordinary Lives, Lived Extraordinarily

There was a time when I would have read about Sr. Blandina
and St. Teresa and said, "They don't make women like that anymore." When I was younger, I often felt that sainthood was not
just elusive but downright unattainable for me. But now these
stories of holy women and brave saints inspire me to live my
own acts of audacity.

Years later, when I discovered Flannery O'Connor's writing, I stumbled across this line in one of her stories: "She could
never be a saint, but she thought she could be a martyr if they
killed her quick." I loved the self-deprecating humor in it, but
more than that, I found a measure of truth that struck home. The
young girl in the story contemplates her faith and all the ways
she's willing to die a martyr's death, while recognizing that
she might not have the strength for a long and lingering death.
I, too, wonder if I have the strength to sustain this long-term
commitment when it gets hard or tedious.

These women were determined and daring, but they also
demonstrated their audacity in the way they conquered the daily
grind. The daily sacrifice. The daily offering of everything boring
and hard. Instead of looking at the circumstances in which these
women lived and trying to replicate their lives, I ought to emulate the traits that made them excellent models of womanhood
and sainthood.

In my rather ordinary life as a college professor, I'm not
likely to stand down a notorious outlaw, but I might encounter a difficult student. I have not taken a vow of obedience to
a mother superior or bishop, but I am bound by professional

ethics to follow policies and develop curriculum and programs according to those policies.

I am more like Sr. Blandina and St. Teresa than I initially thought. They were ordinary women who did extraordinary things for the love of God. These women did amazing things because they tackled *acts of love,* whether it was providing medical care to a wounded outlaw or leadership to correct a community's lax ways.

I am inspired to see where I can commit to living my life full of audacious acts of love. At home I can create a space that is welcoming and pleasant for my family and guests. At work I can do the same to create an environment of welcome, with attention to detail in completing my duties. When I see this as an expression of love, I feel I can accomplish anything, small or great, for the glory of God.

Can it be that simple? The path to sainthood starts—and ends—with my desire to act for the love of God.

I think I can do that. I know I can, as countless saints have done before me. It'll just take a little audacity on my part to make that commitment daily. I need to banish the silly notion that "they don't make women like that anymore."

Of course God does.

questions to ponder

1. Define *audacity.* Name a woman in your life who fits your definition. How does she exemplify audacious living?

2. Recall a time in your life when you did something audacious. Were you successful? Were you brave or frightened? Or both? How did that make you feel?

3. What bold step can you take in your spiritual life? Is there a devotion you might want to add to your routine? A chaplet? A Rosary? Do you feel called to consider a consecration to Jesus through Mary?

Commit an act of audacity in your spiritual life.

chapter two

courageous soldiers who fought real, meaningful battles

Nancy Wake and St. Joan of Arc

You must do the thing you think you cannot do.

~Eleanor Roosevelt

In high school, the unit on World War II came alive for me because my history teacher, Mr. Davis, was a veteran of the war. He was an unassuming, soft-spoken gentleman right up until we got to that unit, when something amazing happened. He opened up and became animated and passionate. It turns out he had served under General Patton's command as an infantryman and had participated in the liberation of Buchenwald concentration camp. He spoke to us in great detail about the experience, and it was chilling to hear a first-person account of the ravages of war. We looked at pictures in the textbook, and he identified obscure little things that we wouldn't have known.

He told us he felt that nothing he had ever done or could possibly ever do would eclipse the moment when he saw the release of the prisoners from the concentration camp.

At that time, in the late 1970s, Miami Beach had a large population of European Jews who had first migrated to the northeastern part of the United States and later sought a calmer, more relaxed retirement in southern Florida. Many Holocaust survivors came to our schools to tell their stories, but most often I encountered them in the ordinary moments of life. They were just regular people living peaceful lives who happened to roll up their sleeves in the Miami heat and expose, unabashedly, tattooed numbers on their forearms.

By now I imagine almost all of them have passed away, but their presence, whether as guests in my school or merely as passing strangers on the street, remains in the images of those serial numbers tattooed in my memory.

Resisting Oppression

World War II was a pivotal event in my family's history. My mother's parents, Spanish Basques, had tried to maintain their ethnic identity in a country that, although not directly involved in the war, conspired against them. The Spanish government was ideologically split between favoring the Allied and Axis forces and in some areas was linked to the Nazis. My family was increasingly in danger: the German *Luftwaffe* periodically bombed towns in northern Spain.

My grandparents fled Spain and made their way to Cuba as refugees, thanks in large part to the efforts of the French Resistance. My grandfather Daniel, a politician in his hometown of Legazpi, was hidden in France. He was led over the Pyrenees mountains by a scout, intending to board a ship bound for Venezuela, where other Spanish Basques were settling in exile. My grandmother Emilia and their firstborn, my aunt Libe, stayed in Legazpi, not knowing whether Daniel was safe or captured or worse. It wasn't safe for her to travel over the mountains with a toddler, and yet it wasn't safe for her to stay behind either, marked as she was as the wife of a Basque politician.

My grandmother must have lived in daily fear, fretting for her life and my aunt's. The bombing had already orphaned more than six thousand Spanish Basque children. My grandmother chose to stay with her daughter, await news of my grandfather's safety, and hope for safe passage out of Spain.

Prayer, I'm sure, sustained her—prayer for courage and fidelity.

A Fight for Life

I have an inkling of the fear my grandmother lived with during that difficult time. When my son was born under duress in what was one moment a normal delivery and the next a mad scramble, my husband and I endured a horrible ordeal; we didn't know what was happening or how our son was doing as the medical team worked to save his little life. After a few terrifying moments, he was stabilized and born with no further incident. But those moments. Those moments! Time slowed down and all I could think was "No! No!" I don't believe I could have articulated a single thought.

My doctor, a man of exemplary faith who often sat in the pew in front of us at church, worked on me and my son quickly, doing what he had to do to stop Jonathan from moving farther into the birth canal and to keep me calm enough to follow his directions.

"Pray! You pray! I'll work."

So I prayed. I couldn't think. I couldn't do anything at all while the nurses worked diligently to prep me; all I could do was ask St. Michael for help. I wasn't even particularly devoted to St. Michael at the time. But my doctor's name was Michael. In fact, his name was the Spanish version of Michael the Archangel—*Miguel Arcangel*. I figured that the one who needed the most intercession right then was the man holding my son's life in his hands. Literally. My son Jonathan's middle name is Michael.

He knows his birth story, of course, and sometimes fools around and gives his name as Michelangelo. He's not wrong.

I've had recourse to St. Michael many times over the years since. I never seem to get past the first line of the prayer, though. I never learned it in English. To me, the first line says it all: *St. Michael the Archangel, defend us in battle. . . .*

A Fight for Dignity

Every day, it seems, we go out and fight a hard battle, don't you think? Over the course of a career spanning three decades, I've had to stand up to an injustice or two, including some serious battles requiring a measure of courage I didn't realize I had until just that moment. I soon discovered that a little righteous indignation can go a long way in fueling the passion necessary for a good fight.

Teaching employability skills to Cuban and Haitian refugees in Little Havana was the most difficult thing I had ever done. I wasn't sheltered or coddled as a child, but I had never seen or experienced what real poverty looked like up close and personal. I had the abstract understanding that poor people lacked money and resources, yet this experience introduced me to the complexity of poverty—what it means to be impoverished in so many areas of life that I had taken for granted.

Many of my clients had no homes. I knew they had no money or jobs. I learned they had no education, no marketable skills. No family or friends. In many cases, no faith—they had a limited understanding or a misunderstanding of their intrinsic value as human beings.

In short, they had no hope.

I thought my job was to teach them how to fill out job applications, but it involved so much more; I had to teach them some of the rudimentary essentials, gently suggesting to men my father's age that they should wash their hands and wear a clean shirt when applying for a job, for example. From one day to the next, I never knew what I would be called upon to do or say. And I cried every single day as I drove through two affluent neighborhoods on my way home from work because I felt powerless to change things.

Over time, cynicism crept in. I realized that many of my clients weren't likely to get jobs, in spite of all my earnest instruction. And if they did get jobs, they'd likely lose them for any of a myriad of reasons that had nothing to do with how well I'd taught them. I was merely one of the boxes they had to check in order to continue receiving aid.

I resisted the bureaucracy and fought the system. First, though, I had to fight my own inclination toward complacency. I saw others just going through the motions of passing along the clients. Would I have what it took to keep teaching? To keep fighting the battle against hopelessness?

It wasn't easy. I was young and inexperienced, in my faith as well as my job skills. I didn't have the greatest source of strength I turn to today, the simple but powerful prayer, *Jesus, I trust in you.*

Still, I got up every morning and met the day's challenge. I endeavored to see every person as a unique individual, not a set of boxes that required my check marks and initials. That's when my real education began.

I learned to hear not just with my ears, but with my intellect and my heart. I could hear the words "I'll take any job that's available" and understand the unspoken part: *but I have small children and no one to leave them with.* If I heard "I forgot my glasses at home" when I gave written instructions for aid, I stopped to read the document to the client before sending him on, certain he was illiterate, not farsighted.

I don't think I saved anyone from poverty in the nine months I worked at the center, but I hope the clients who saw me knew that I saw *them.* I hope they received from me some measure of validation of their intrinsic worth as human beings made in the image of the Creator. I know the experience formed me in the way I would teach for decades to come.

These days when I pray "St. Michael the Archangel, defend us in battle; be our protection against the wickedness and snares of the devil," my battles are in the classrooms and halls of academe—in the workplace, not the streets. These are the battles most of us are likely to face today, even though on the world stage we're seeing carnage and violence and the mass destruction and genocide of people everywhere.

Those battles require a different kind of courage, the kind that soldiers and freedom fighters call upon. I don't know that I have the strength for such battles, but then again maybe I do—maybe I just haven't needed it so far. My grandfather, met with necessity, put his trust in a guide and traveled through the mountains in a war zone.

The White Mouse

The first time I heard the story of the French Resistance leader code-named the White Mouse by the Nazi SS intelligence forces, I wondered if I had a personal connection to her—perhaps she had played a role in saving the lives of my grandparents.

Nancy Wake, an Australian socialite who married a French businessman at the onset of World War II, began working as a spy when her husband was recruited by the French Resistance. She was an ideal candidate for delivering information to outposts scattered throughout France and the bordering Mediterranean countries. After all, a French businessman's beautiful young wife couldn't possibly pose a problem to anyone.

It was the perfect cover, and Wake used it to her advantage. She commanded more than three thousand men in the French Resistance bands called the Maquis, attaining the rank of captain and ultimately the title Chevalier de la Légion d'Honneur. Her heroic actions earned her many distinguished service medals, including the Croix de Guerre, the Médaille de la Résistance, and the United States Medal of Freedom.

Wake was so elusive that the Nazis named her the White Mouse; they were never able to identify her. The last person they would suspect as a spy was this beauty who was clearly interested only in spas and shopping, inconveniently interrupted now by a raging war. The perfect cover was . . . well . . . perfect. Her beauty, while legendary among the men under her command, was nothing compared to her courage and grit in the face of the dangers she encountered in the field. She did some violent things in her position, not just rising to the occasion, but excelling in it.

Two remarkable stories about Nancy Wake stand out and speak to me as a woman. The first one, which shows her strength and dedication to duty, revolves around what in today's work-force might amount to sexual harassment. She would have none of it. Parachuting into a hostile area of Auvergne in France filled with enemy operatives, she landed in a tree and got tangled up in the branches. One of the men had to cut her down. As he was working to release the hanging Wake, he asked her if all the trees in France had such beautiful fruit hanging from them. Irritated by his forward manner, she told him to cut out "that French shit."

Captain Wake was clearly a force to be reckoned with, as that man discovered. I imagine once she came down out of the tree he stood at attention and saluted her before rejoining his unit. I like that story about her; although there are plenty of sto-ries about her valor in the field, this personal interaction reveals her ability to command respect from the troops she was lead-ing. Wake volunteered for this mission. She might have been recruited, but she still had to give her assent, her *yes*. She fought a meaningful battle, and it was not without personal loss and sacrifice.

While on a break from their dangerous work, she and her husband were reunited and enjoying some much-needed time to reconnect. His contribution to the Resistance centered around his business relationships, and early in the fighting he would disappear on missions and then return. This time, they were both called at the same time to participate in covert missions. He disappeared, and she was called into deeper covert acts. She did not discover he had been killed until after the war. During all that time, she remained faithful to him, hoping he would even-tually surface. Although she was a formidable woman—intel-ligent, powerful, and as was often noted, quite beautiful—she remained faithful to her husband and their vows until she had confirmation of his death.

Her courage and fidelity in the face of danger make Nancy Wake the kindred spirit of another woman—a canonized saint who during her short life fought valiantly the battles she believed God had called her to fight.

Courage and Fidelity

Centuries before Nancy Wake was being plucked from a tree in Auvergne, another woman took up the standard of war to fight just north of those fields, not for the liberation of France, but for its unification.

Jeanne d'Arc (Joan of Arc) was born on January 6, 1412, in Domrémy, France, during the time of the Hundred Years' War. Prolonged political division in the country had resulted in an unresolved claim to the throne. Two feuding factions arose: the Burgundians, who supported the Duke of Burgundy and were allied with the English, and the Armagnacs, who acknowledged Charles VII as king of France. Joan's village had been burned down in the conflict, and the inhabitants lived under the threat of more destruction.

Despite this unrest, Joan had a normal childhood. She was the youngest of five children in a peasant family. Her father, Jacques, owned his own land and was dedicated to farming and raising cattle. Joan, while not educated formally, probably learned the same skills that girls her age mastered: spinning, sewing, and tending to the household chores when she wasn't helping her father during plantings and harvests. She also had a love of the poor. Records indicate that she was quite pious and spent a great deal of her time in prayer at the church.

From the time she was thirteen, Joan had remarkable visions of St. Michael, St. Margaret of Antioch, and St. Catherine of Alexandria that led her to believe that she was receiving divine guidance. Joan refused to describe what transpired in her visions, saying only that she was bidden to speak to the dauphin (Charles's title as heir to the throne) and to hasten his coronation. Although she was barely a teenager at the time, Joan accepted this charge. She attempted to meet with Charles on several occasions but was foiled by the men in his court. Finally, Lord Robert

Baudricourt, commander of Charles's army near Vaucouleurs, became convinced of Joan's mission when she predicted accurately that the army would suffer a loss near Orléans.

Baudricourt took her to see Charles immediately, but then the dauphin needed convincing. She was able to do so by revealing to him his personal prayer petitions. These astounding revelations stirred up suspicion and fear. In each case her piety and trust in God, as well as her fealty and dedication to France, convinced her detractors. Joan's counsel in the war rooms and presence on the battlefield, holding up the standard for all to see and take comfort in, led to many victories and, finally, to the coronation of Charles VII as rightful king of France.

Tragically, the rest of her story is consumed by political maneuvering, a lack of support for her holy influence, and unfounded accusations of heresy that resulted in a heavily biased trial and death sentence. Joan of Arc was burned at the stake. She was only nineteen.

Almost thirty years later, at the behest of her mother, Pope Callixtus III authorized a retrial that reversed the earlier decision. Joan was declared innocent and a martyr for the faith. In 1920, after hundreds of years, she was canonized by Pope Benedict XV.

Both Nancy Wake and St. Joan of Arc stood for justice and the belief that a better world was possible. Wake followed her convictions to help end war of aggression in Europe, and St. Joan of Arc followed God's will as it was revealed to her through three powerful saints. Both women showed courage and fidelity in the face of danger. We can all learn from their example to carry our standards courageously into the battles we face.

questions to ponder

1. Define *courage*. Name a woman in your life who fits your definition. How does she exemplify courageous living?
2. Recall a time in your life when you did something courageous. What was the outcome? How did that make you feel?

3. Where in your spiritual life do you need courage? Have you
    been away from the sacraments and do you want to return?
    Do you desire to make a deeper commitment to the Lord?

Take one courageous step in response to Christ's call.

missionary adventurers
who had a heart for the world

Edel Quinn and St. Helena

Faith is strengthened when it is given to others!

~Pope John Paul II, *Redemptoris Missio*

It turns out I'm a missionary. It's not something I ever aspired to—it just happened.

One evening more than ten years ago I received a call from a friend. He was excited to share some new technology with me and thought I'd be a kind critic. He sent me an Internet link to an audio file called a podcast, explaining that "it's like a radio show, only you listen to it on the Internet whenever you want." He wanted me to listen and tell him what I thought.

I thought it was tinny sounding and a strange way for a grown man to spend an evening. It reminded me of the days when as kids we'd tape-record ourselves cutting up on cassette decks—the kind where you had to press the record button and the play button at the same time and speak into the tiny internal microphone on the top corner of the case. I pretty much outgrew that by the time I was ten.

At the time, I wondered to myself, "Who would want to listen to a podcast *on purpose?*" As it turns out . . . thousands of people did. The friend was Greg Willits, and the podcast was the first episode of *Rosary Army Podcast,* which went on to become one of the most popular podcasts in Catholic new media. (I'm glad my saying it sounded tinny didn't discourage him too much!) Greg and his wife, Jennifer, went on to host *Rosary Army Podcast* for many years and eventually created their own radio show, *The Catholics Next Door.*

Missionaries without the Mosquitoes

Greg was on fire for the Lord and full of creative ideas. I met him and his young family at our parish. I taught his oldest son in the children's liturgy, and he showed my oldest daughter how to make twine rosaries on a teen retreat. That retreat led to the creation of Rosary Army, a lay apostolate dedicated to making, praying, and giving away twine rosaries. Eventually, I joined their board of directors and Greg invited me to write for the website. That led to one of the most inspiring collaborations I've ever participated in: cowriting *That Catholic Show,* the video series he produced with Jennifer.

We spent many afternoons in a local coffee shop hashing out episodes of this popular show. I learned how to pitch ideas and how to take criticism—*especially how to take criticism.* I don't think I've ever had my work slashed and cut up and sent back to the drawing board like in those days. It was the most fun I've ever had writing.

By then, I had already followed Greg and Jennifer over to another apostolate with a Dutch podcasting priest, Fr. Roderick Vonhögen. Fr. Roderick created the Star Quest Podcasting Network (SQPN) in the Netherlands after producing some behind-the-scenes podcast reporting of Pope John Paul II's final days. Since he was studying at the Vatican, Fr. Roderick took his portable recorder everywhere and developed what he eventually called a "sound-seeing tour." The *New York Times* picked up news of his podcast, and *Catholic Insider* took off. I became a board member of the organization in its early years and remained through the rebranding of the apostolate to Star Quest Production Network. I was delighted to work with Fr. Roderick on the popular podcast *The Secrets of Harry Potter*, contributing my expertise in the field of literature to the analysis of the fantasy series.

At first I didn't consider the work I was doing through Rosary Army and SQPN to be missionary work. To be honest my stereotype of a missionary was Katharine Hepburn in *The African Queen*. Missionaries go into isolated places and fight malaria-carrying mosquitoes while evangelizing people about the Good Word, and I hate mosquitoes. I do like my friends though, especially getting together to talk with my friends. Because I cannot separate my Catholic faith from who I am, everything I do has an inherent Catholic element to it. This is probably true of every faithful Catholic I know, whether or not they are walking around wearing a huge Miraculous Medal or carrying a breviary.

This means that in the course of any conversation, I am just as likely to talk about standing in line at the grocery store or seeing the latest superhero movie as I am to mention forgetting it's Friday and ordering a hamburger at lunch. These things are a part of my life. *Catholic Weekend*, my talk show, captures that organic relationship between real life and the Catholic faith. We're a group of friends who get together on Saturday mornings to catch up on our week and discuss current events through a Catholic lens. We joke about having a loose organizational structure for the episodes, but we've never pretended to be a slick show. On the contrary, we just try to be true to our faith and enjoy each other's company while demonstrating that faithful Catholics are real people. It resonates with an audience that's walking that faith journey alongside us. We're all trying to maneuver in a world that makes living the faith a challenge at best and frustrating in some of the more difficult moments.

Somewhere along the way I realized that this is a twenty-first-century model of missionary work. Instead of pith helmets, we wear headsets. Instead of hiking books and ground guides, we use laptops and microphones. We're still taking the Good Word out into isolated places—we just don't have to worry about mosquitoes.

An Evangelizing Superhero without a Cape

Edel Quinn *did* have to worry about mosquitoes—she eventually contracted malaria. She didn't walk on water, but she once convinced a priest to drive across a bridge that had been breached in a flood because the Blessed Virgin Mary wouldn't want them to be late to a meeting. I admire that plucky attitude.

I'd say Edel was a little crazy, except that everything in her life points to one truth: she was committed to Jesus through his mother, Mary, and nothing else mattered. *Nothing else mattered.* I don't have that kind of detachment. Oh, I can find it in rare moments, but to live my entire life like that? That's heroic. And Edel Quinn did it.

I first learned about Edel through the Legion of Mary. My devotion to the Rosary led me to a number of resources about this powerful prayer, and there was Edel, featured on the Legion of Mary website. I was struck by her unusual name, and years later, I rediscovered Edel because I read a blog post about ten Catholic women who changed the world. There was Edel Quinn in a list that included St. Therese of Lisieux and Mother Teresa. I had to learn more about this woman of influence.

Edel Mary Quinn was born in County Cork, Ireland, in 1907. Her father was a banker, and the family moved around quite a bit in her youth. She had decided as a young girl to pursue the religious life and join the Poor Clares. Unfortunately, Edel contracted tuberculosis as a young woman. She spent almost two years in a sanatorium, but she never quite recovered. Unable to join the sisters, Edel instead joined the Legion of Mary, a recently formed lay apostolate that served the poor in Dublin.

At the age of twenty, Edel dedicated herself completely to the work of this new organization. The Legion of Mary broke ground in its approach and served as a model for what laypeople could do; the members dedicated themselves to actively living their baptismal promises in fraternity and prayer for the conversion of the world.

I feel the same way about my work in new media. Rosary Army and SQPN broke ground in using new media for the New Evangelization. We do the same thing Edel and her companions did—we just use different tools.

Edel became very real to me. I could understand her dedication to the apostolate's mission of prayer and active cooperation in the work of the Church; I, too, have a deep love for Our Lady and am grateful for her gentle and kind presence in my life, leading me always to her Son. I was emboldened to learn that Edel was committed to her fellow legionaries in much the same way I treasure the friendships I've made over time through Rosary Army and SQPN. What struck me, though, was Edel's commitment to the Legion's work in making sure its mission got carried out everywhere she could take it.

Edel was dying of tuberculosis. Her time in the sanatorium had not helped her condition, so she decided to press forward in God's work anyway. She was not yet thirty years old when she became an envoy of the Legion of Mary and accepted the challenge of becoming a missionary in Africa. By the end of 1936, Edel had traveled to Mombasa, Kenya, and settled in Nairobi for what would become one of the most astounding examples of missionary work in the early part of the twentieth century. Edel established hundreds of branches of the Legion of Mary throughout eastern and central Africa, all while suffering from tuberculosis and the complications brought on by malaria. The effects of her work can be seen today in the thousands of Catholic faithful throughout Africa.

Although Edel had physical limitations that led to several health crises, her stalwart faith in God never wavered. With the Eucharist at the center of her life and faith, Edel could do anything. She faced terrible trials as she made her way across unknown areas of the African continent, traveling in a beat-up Ford and trusting in a driver who, as a Muslim, did not share her faith. She encountered racial prejudice as well, but never let that be a cause for discouragement. Instead, Edel put her trust in God, saying, "We can never love too much; let us give utterly and not count the cost. God will respond to our faith in him."

Edel was often seen with a rosary in her hand and a smile on her face. Joy, it seems, was an ever-present grace. She exuded total confidence that Mary would take care of everything, and was often known to remark she could not refuse Mary anything.

After almost eight years of dedication as a missionary, Edel succumbed to the ravages of tuberculosis and died quietly in Nairobi in 1944. She is buried in the missionaries' cemetery there. In 1956, a cause for canonization was opened, and in 1984, Pope John Paul II declared Edel Mary Quinn venerable.

Edel completed her missionary adventure in a small window of time and died at the young age of thirty-six. She demonstrated, as have so many saints before her, that youth is not a liability but one of the greatest assets of the Church. Her witness to the faith, though brief, inspires me today.

In a very real way, Edel had a heart for the world, a Christ-centered love that compelled her to endure whatever was necessary in order to proclaim the Gospel to those who most needed to hear it. In that way she reminds me a great deal of another intrepid traveler: St. Helena, mother of the fourth-century Roman emperor Constantine.

A Generous Missionary Pilgrim

St. Helena of Constantinople, known for uncovering the True Cross in Jerusalem, did her greatest work in the last years of her long and exciting life. St. Helena was less of a missionary like Edel, though, and more of a *missionary pilgrim*. She journeyed to places where Christianity was already established and worked to strengthen it, often providing monetary support and, on several occasions, building churches.

Her early life showed no sign that she would become the most powerful woman in her era. Born sometime in the middle of the third century into a poor family, Helena was probably a

stable girl when Constantius, a Roman general, took her as his
wife. She bore him a son, Constantine.

Constantius divorced Helena in order to make a more poli-
tic marriage for himself on the way to becoming emperor. Helena
was sent away, but maintained a loving relationship with her
son. In AD 306 Constantius died and his son Constantine rose
to the office of emperor. He immediately summoned his mother
and established her in a position of great honor as the mother
of the sovereign.

Constantine, also known as Constantine the Great or, more
significantly, *Saint* Constantine, exerted a powerful influence
over his mother, especially late in her life. The powerful Roman
Empire had been cruel to Christians in those first centuries following the establishment of the Church. St. Constantine reversed
the treatment of Christians in AD 313 by proclaiming freedom
of worship for all religions. This not only made it legal to be
Christian but also allowed Christianity to gain a stronghold
in the Roman Empire. According to tradition, he had a powerful conversion after seeing a vision of a cross emblazoned with
the words "In this sign, conquer." Twelve years after declaring
himself a Christian, in 325 Constantine called the First Council
of Nicaea, where the Nicene Creed was affirmed. In a reversal
from the usual story of parents influencing and educating their
children, in this case it was Constantine who showed his mother
the way to Christ.

These events, and Constantine's holy influence, led to a
profound conversion for Helena. As a Christian, she now used
her power and influence to help spread Christianity throughout the empire. Her piety and zealousness for the faith were
renowned. So was her charity: Helena had a special love for the
poor and did much to help them through her unique position.
Perhaps, having come from poverty, she understood this need
well. Because of her position, St. Helena also had inexhaustible
resources to apply toward her quest to discover Christian relics,
the most famous of all, of course, being the True Cross.

St. Helena built numerous churches in the Holy Land. Even
though she was already in her seventies, Helena undertook a

trip to Palestine, where she visited every single site she could see, tracing Christ's footsteps. It was, no doubt, a meaningful experience for her, but her desire to show God both gratitude and devotion prompted her to give generously to the communities she encountered.

St. Helena's actions inspire me because of the nature of her giving. She was certainly in a position to be financially generous, but often that can be accomplished at a distance. Instead, Helena went to the Holy Land and other places within the Roman Empire and saw for herself what the needs were, whether personal or for the greater community.

The finding of the True Cross occurred as a result of St. Helena's benevolence and her love of Christ. She wanted the whole world to experience him, but more than that, she wanted him to receive proper praise and worship. Everywhere Helena visited she shared this rich, pious zeal for the Lord.

With her son's support, St. Helena authorized the building of the Church of the Nativity in Bethlehem, as well as the beautification of other churches such as that on the Mount of Olives. Her desire for beautification carried over into projects to clean up much of the clutter and destruction in the Holy Land left from Emperor Hadrian's destruction of Jerusalem. It was during one of these projects that, according to legend, three crosses were discovered. St. Helena, convinced that one must be the cross on which Jesus was crucified, had an ill woman brought to her. The woman was given a piece of each cross to hold, and when she touched the last one and was cured, St. Helena knew it to be the True Cross.

We're All Missionary Pilgrims

It's difficult to separate facts from legend in the lives of saints of the early days of the Church. However, the stories do capture the larger truth about the pious dedication of people who lived before us. When I read about a courageous woman such as Edel Quinn, who lived mere decades before me, I am encouraged to know that there are saints in the making in my world. Edel's life was documented well by the people who worked with her. On the other hand, perhaps all the stories surrounding St. Helena are exaggerations or metaphorical depictions of a holy life.

What matters to me in the lives of these women is their commitment to spread the faith. I admire Edel's missionary heart and demonstration of her trust in God. She dedicated her *entire self,* despite her severe illness, to spreading God's love into areas of the world where her witness bore much fruit. St. Helena endured the trials of travel in the fourth century to bear witness to the suffering of Christians in her time and to bring consolation through her pious support of Christian communities.

I love the idea of the missionary pilgrim. One of the things I've learned from my own faith journey is how much it enriches me to share my faith with others. Of course I learn new things as I prepare to teach, but even in the spontaneous moments when I get caught up in a conversation or make a conscious effort to choose charity over selfishness, I grow in my faith and my love of God, as I'm sure Edel Quinn and St. Helena did on their holy adventures.

questions to ponder

1. Define *missionary*, not only in the sense of traveling overseas, but in the sense of sharing Jesus with those who do not know him. Name a woman in your life who fits your definition. How does she exemplify a missionary life?

2. Recall a time in your life when you spread the Good News. How was it received? How did that make you feel?

3. What part of your spiritual life do you want to share with others? Do you enjoy leading group prayer such as a Rosary or chaplet? Do you have a special skill or love of a devotion that you would like to share with others?

Be a shining light of Christ's love to others as you go about your day.

~~~~~~~~~~~~~~~~~~~~~~~~~~~~

outspoken advocates
who challenged the status quo

Mother Mary Lange and St. Catherine of Siena

~~~~~~~~~~~~~~~~~~~~~~~~~~~~

Proclaim the truth and do not be silent through fear.

~St. Catherine of Siena

I learned how to negotiate successfully when I was about five years old. Although I had a room full of toys, I got my mother to buy me a cheap little ball on one of her shopping trips to the local Kmart. No doubt I badgered her, promising to clean my room or share my toys with my little brother until she gave in. Who knew that I was developing my advocacy skills at such a young age? It served me well in the coming years when I had to face something other than a flighty desire.

When I was a little girl, if I accompanied my mother to the store, which was usually *every time* she went to the store, she'd let me play in the toy section until the shopping was done. How times have changed! But in those days, I probably made friends with another little kid and we played until our mothers came to collect us.

My favorite game was tossing balls into the open top of a wire cage that contained two or three dozen balls. There was an opening on the bottom, and I'd grab a ball and toss it over the top, grab another ball, and do the same. I could do this for hours. Sometimes I'd keep a count of how many balls I had successfully tossed back into the cage, and then try to break my record next time.

When my mother bought me the ball I had coveted so much, I took it home and treasured it. It was my favorite possession for a while, probably until I got a Spirograph or a View-Master. Until then, though, the ball was the thing. It had a blue swirly design on a white background. The seam where the two sides were sealed together was a little off, which made the ball difficult to bounce in a straight line. I didn't care and soon learned to compensate for its wobbly design so that I could bounce the ball in place and then actually dribble it on the run like a basketball player. I was pretty impressive for a little kid.

I spent many afternoons dribbling in the development's parking lot and shooting at an imaginary basket by the big dumpster. If I threw the ball into the corner and hit the dark blue box next to the latch, I counted it as a basket.

Life as a five-year-old was good.

Then my playmates, the daughters of some of my parents' friends, started ballet lessons. They looked cute in their pink tights and ballet slippers, so I wanted to take ballet lessons, too.

My father said no. Just like that. I didn't think to challenge him, not at age five. I went back to dribbling. That fall, my parents enrolled me in the Mighty Mites basketball league at my elementary school, and soon I was playing with my age group for our practices and games and sneaking off to the big kids' baskets, where I strained mightily to get the ball up near the basket. Eventually, I was strong enough to hit the rim or backboard, and accuracy followed pretty quickly. By the end of the season, I was playing in both age brackets and having a blast.

That was the beginning of my very long love affair with the game of basketball. I didn't give ballet another thought. I spent the next few years on the court, always stretching myself, always wanting to play against the boys who were bigger and faster. Playing above my skill level improved my game, and I became a very good and competitive player.

Challenging the Status Quo

One day, when I was about fifteen or sixteen, my little sister came home in pink tights and ballet slippers. My parents had enrolled her in ballet classes. Full-strength teenage defiance burst out of my mouth as I challenged my parents with the unfair treatment I had received. I mean, I had wanted to dance and they hadn't let me. And now my little sister got to dance. I'm sure I whined that it wasn't fair.

My dad listened to me carry on for a while and then asked simply, "Did you ever dance around the house? Did you ever walk around on your tippy toes?"

"No," I replied.

"*No*," he repeated. "You dribbled that annoying ball in every room."

True. I never said another word about ballet. That day I learned the difference between equity and equality. I thought I wanted *equality*—to have the very same thing my sister had—when in fact what I wanted, what I really needed, and what I had received was *equity*—the fair and just opportunity to pursue what I loved. And my sister had the very same opportunity to pursue what she loved.

I learned a lot of other lessons while playing basketball, most of them on the court: Teamwork. Persistence. Drive. I learned to face adversity and come out a winner, regardless of the numbers on the scoreboard. The court was a great equalizer for me. Nobody cared that I had a funny name. It didn't matter that I was socially awkward and didn't have the cool shoes or wear the right reptile on my sweater. I could pass the basketball with speed and dexterity, and my shots hit the sweet spot just about every time.

My skill on the court didn't make me popular, but it did make me a leader. I became captain my junior year, and it carried over into my senior year. As captain, I could speak on behalf of the team, schedule team activities, even give a few motivational talks at halftime. Although I preferred to lie low and just play the game, sometimes I had to confront the bias against female athletes. I didn't like confrontation; I still don't. But sometimes challenging the status quo is the right thing to do. I wasn't a fan of fighting authority for the sake of change, but as a female athlete coming of age on the heels of Title IX legislation, I faced a small battle every time I walked onto the court, whether I wanted it that way or not.

Title IX endeavored to bring equity to sports access for girls. Most of the school's athletic funds were used to grow existing football and basketball programs for the boys. To be honest, those were also the sports that generated income for the athletic program. There was some resistance from male coaches and players alike and a lot of negative attitude when, for example, the gym schedule prioritized girls' varsity practice over boys' junior varsity practice. Equipment, locker rooms, uniforms—all of these came under scrutiny.

As captain of the girls' varsity basketball team, I was under scrutiny, too. If I challenged the administration for slights, both real and perceived, then I was considered a troublemaker. If I didn't challenge the administration, my teammates accused me of not caring about the team—and I felt I was not being true to myself.

The experience served me well. I learned to communicate my position clearly, establish what I wanted, and compromise. I learned to represent my interests, but also to speak on behalf of a group. I learned to accept defeat on and *off* the court with grace, but more importantly, to win with grace. That was the harder of the two. I was lucky, *blessed*, to have two exceptional coaches who modeled leadership for me and supported me in those endeavors.

Over time, I discovered other spiritual mentors who, like those coaches, challenged the status quo and encouraged me to speak my mind in the pursuit of justice, a challenge I've faced throughout my professional life working in education and community services. I found in women like Mother Mary Lange and St. Catherine of Siena a gritty determination to act for justice that helped me develop the integrity to pursue change, whether in policies or attitudes, because it was the right thing to do—the moral choice, not the convenient choice.

A Pioneering Educator of the Neglected

I am drawn to stories of women who face adversity or challenges and are not afraid to set about making things right, without a lot of fanfare or attention. The world has plenty of over-the-top headlines; I like to hear about people who just go about doing their jobs. Their example gives me a sense of encouragement that I can effect meaningful change in small, fulfilling ways.

The story of Mother Mary Lange surprised me. I feel a deep kinship with this woman through our similar multigenerational immigration stories that ultimately brought us both to the United States, though in different times and to different cities.

Of French and African descent, she was born Elizabeth Clarisse Lange in Santiago de Cuba in 1784. Other oral traditions indicate she may have been born in Haiti. Her family fled the violence and uncertainty of the Haitian Revolution, emigrating first to southeastern Cuba in one of Santiago's French-speaking neighborhoods and ultimately to Baltimore, Maryland, in 1812.

This was, of course, prior to the abolition of slavery. Although there were many free African Americans living in Baltimore at the turn of the century, educational opportunities for black children remained limited, with no formal public schools available, only private schools.

Having settled into an area of Baltimore where many Haitian refugees lived, Lange found that Haitian children had no recourse for an education. Together with a friend, Lange used her inheritance to open and operate a free school for them out of her home. She was soon approached by a local priest, Sulpician Father James Joubert, a Frenchman who had also fled the political unrest in Haiti. Fr. Joubert noted that the children in his catechism classes could not read or write in English. He shared with Lange his dream of establishing for the girls in the community a Church-supported school run by religious sisters.

Lange was immediately open to the idea, expressing to Fr. Joubert that she had desired to serve God for many years, but had been unable to because the religious life was not open to women of color in that era. Eventually, with the blessing of Baltimore's Archbishop James Whitfield, they founded the first order of African American religious sisters, the Oblate Sisters of Providence.

In 1828, they opened the Oblate School for Colored Girls with only nine students and several novices. Taking the name Mary, Lange professed her vows in 1829 and became the first mother superior of the Oblate Sisters of Providence. By 1853, the school had undergone expansions and moves, exponential growth, and a name change to St. Frances Academy. The school still exists today!

Mother Mary Lange's influence soon extended beyond that free classroom in her home. Mother Lange and the sisters taught school, provided vocational training, led literacy programs, and visited the poor. They also provided a safe environment for a group of orphaned black children after the Civil War. "We only seek to do the will of God," she explained.

With her humility and desire to fulfill God's plan for her, Mother Lange serves as a wonderful model of virtue. Recently declared Servant of God because of the work she and her sisters accomplished, Mother Lange endured the trials of racial injustice and extreme poverty for the sake of the children she educated and the community she loved. Her advocacy for these children truly served the needs of her time.

Sometimes I'm afraid to take risks, especially if I encounter resistance. I most often face this in my work as it relates to student success. I know the change I want and the support I need, but challenging the system can create resentments or even hostility. I struggle with the fear of the unknown consequences of advocating for what is right.

And so I am encouraged by women like Mother Mary Lange, who was not afraid to name an injustice and work to rectify society's error in not providing educational opportunities to all children, and the equally bold St. Catherine of Siena, who told a pope to get back to Rome to do his job. Both of these women knew, as St. Catherine once observed, that "nothing great is ever achieved without much enduring." Mother Mary Lange endured by trusting in God's will for his children; centuries earlier, St. Catherine bravely challenged the status quo with integrity as she pressed for reform and peace. Both of these women, through their words and deeds, encourage me to do the same.

An Ambassador with a Cause

Catherine was born in 1347 in Siena, Italy, and died just thirty-three years later in Rome. She was declared a Doctor of the Church in 1970 for her extensive collection of letters, her *Dialogue,* and her collection of prayers. She is recognized for her deeply spiritual and mystical writing.

I was astounded to discover that St. Catherine struggled to learn how to read and write, something she accomplished only in adulthood. I love to share that with my students—adults facing the same challenge.

Catherine appealed to me because she believed there had to be more opportunities for women besides marriage or the convent. She refused marriage, having consecrated her life to Jesus, which left her with few options. While I never fully embraced feminism as so many women my age did, I didn't entirely reject it either. I had too much of the traditional old-country upbringing to accept it, but enough of the rebel in me to seek my own independence. Those years of playing sports and trying to rise above the fray in the boys-versus-girls conflicts of my high school years left a mark: I had a bit of a chip on my shoulder when it came to challenging the status quo. I still do, and I willingly share my opinion when asked, even if it is unpopular.

St. Catherine's life was extraordinary, if brief. She was born into the wealthy Benincasa family, which already had twenty-two children, half of whom had died; Catherine's twin sister, Giovanna, also died shortly after birth. (Two years later, her mother had a twenty-fifth child, whom she also named Giovanna.) The Black Death had devastated that part of the world, and few families were spared its ravages. Yet Catherine was a sweet and joyful little girl who had visions of angels and Jesus from the time she was five or six years old. Her nickname was Euphrosyne, the Greek word for "joy." Her merry temperament would serve her well in later years when she took care of the afflicted during an outbreak of the plague. She ministered to the sick with such joy and tenderness that she witnessed many powerful conversions.

When she turned eighteen, Catherine decided to join the Third Order of St. Dominic. Her parents had wanted her to get married, but Catherine resisted by cutting off her long hair and taking up prolonged periods of fasting. In time her family softened on the issue of marriage and allowed her to live her life as a consecrated virgin, though not in the cloister but at home in silent retreat from the world (and especially from her family).

At age twenty-one, Catherine experienced mystical marriage, a union of her soul to Christ to more intimately share in his suffering. The experience changed her, and she subsequently dedicated herself to the service of the poor and sick. She left the isolation of her rooms in order to carry out her new purpose. This movement back into the world opened her eyes to the unrest in Siena and throughout the country between the various Italian republics and city-states and the Holy See. St. Catherine had a deep dedication to the poor and an amazing spirituality that included visions and mystical occurrences. Nevertheless, it was her involvement in fourteenth-century Italian politics that intrigued me.

I didn't think women had a voice in that era. But St. Catherine not only had a voice . . . she knew how to use it. By the time Catherine was in her late twenties, she had a robust correspondence with a wide circle of influence that included political figures and others in authority. When an uprising against the Holy See, which was in Avignon, France, became imminent, Catherine went as Florence's ambassador to Avignon in 1376 to petition for peace. She endeavored to influence a nonviolent resolution between the republics in Italy and the Holy See. She then met with Pope Gregory XI to petition for the return of the papacy from Avignon back to Rome, reminding him sternly that he had committed to that move . While her efforts to make peace between Florence and the Papal States failed, the following year Pope Gregory did return to Rome! The young woman who had once retreated to the privacy of her rooms under her father's protection was now an adviser to popes, and they listened to her.

Tensions between the Holy See and Florence continued, and Catherine was almost assassinated in riots that broke out after Pope Gregory's death in 1378. She made it out safely and went home to Florence, whence she was summoned by the new pope, Urban VI. At that time, a great schism rocked the Church. Pope Urban VI displeased the cardinals who had elected him, and many of them fled from Rome and elected Robert of Geneva as pope. He took the name of Clement VII and returned to Avignon, effectively becoming an antipope and dividing the Church. The Western Schism, as it became known, was not resolved until decades after St. Catherine's death.

Nevertheless, St. Catherine dedicated the rest of her life to working for the reform of the clergy in support of Pope Urban VI. St. Catherine was respected for taking a stand against the rival factions and the damage being perpetrated against Christ's Church. She was unafraid to speak the truth to those who held the reins of political and ecclesiastical power.

Setting the World Ablaze

St. Catherine corresponded with powerful religious and political figures, exerting holy influence on world events in her lifetime; Mother Mary Lange worked to provide opportunities for disenfranchised people in her community, demonstrating unwavering integrity in the face of tribulations. The lives of both these women speak to me across the centuries, cutting off my fear of my own inadequacies. In the words of St. Catherine: "If you are what you should be, you will set the whole world ablaze!"

She's right. Had I pushed to become a dancer because others were doing it, I would have missed being me. My gift was playing basketball, and through my experiences with the game I gained confidence and a skill set that has enabled me to advocate for and serve the clients and students I've encountered over the years.

Now, I don't think I've set the *whole* world ablaze all by myself. But if I keep the fire burning and touch the lives of a few people . . . and *they* touch a few more people, and so on, soon the whole world will indeed blaze with the love and light of Christ!

Are you in?

questions to ponder

1. Define *advocacy*. Name a woman in your life who fits your definition. How does she exemplify advocacy for a worthy cause?
2. Recall a time in your life when you spoke the truth about an unjust situation. What was the outcome? How did that make you feel?
3. Do you recognize an individual or group in your community in need of a voice? Is there a situation that needs to be addressed lovingly?

Speak the truth. Be an advocate for positive change.

~~~~~~

valiant women who lived and died to uphold human dignity

Phyllis Bowman and St. Gianna Beretta Molla

~~~~~~

Let us love the Cross and let us remember that we are not alone in carrying it. God is helping us. And in God who is comforting us, as St. Paul says, we can do anything.

~St. Gianna Beretta Molla

I grew up watching *M*A*S*H*, the long-running sitcom set in a field hospital in Korea in the 1950s. I enjoyed the pathos of the show—both the writers' ability to strike at the heart of truth and the comedic elements they slipped into the undercurrent of pain. The writers knew some subjects should be treated with the utmost respect, and they had a gift for keeping pain and humor in balance.

I try to strike that balance in my life, especially when happiness seems not only temporary, but fleeting. In those moments of stifled happiness I sometimes get a glimpse of something greater, the unexpected simple beauty of grace in my life. Such a revelation came to me on a midnight ambulance ride to the large military hospital about an hour away from where John and I lived while he was stationed in Germany.

We were spending a quiet night at home, watching television and trying to keep cozy and warm on a freezing winter night. I was pregnant and on bed rest because of some light spotting I'd reported to my obstetrician a few days earlier. His response—a pat on the hand and orders to put my feet up—had done nothing to allay my sense of foreboding, but there had been nothing to do but go home. The doctor had dismissed my symptoms as nothing more than the jitters of a first-time mom. Nevertheless, John had been called back from the field since I was alone. Thousands of miles away from our families, we could only cling to each other over the next several days. And wait.

Things took a turn for the worse that night, and we rushed to the post dispensary, which was more field hospital than ER. I was desolate and probably in shock. I knew I had miscarried, and my heart was wedged somewhere between hopelessness and helplessness. John led me from our home to the car, from the car to the wheelchair, and finally to a sterile room with blinding lights and hushed conversation behind half-drawn curtains.

Remembering the Presence of God

The IV dripped ice into my veins, but I didn't feel any of it. Before I knew what was happening, I was bundled under several layers of green wool blankets and raised into a waiting army ambulance. It was like a scene out of one of those episodes of *M*A*S*H*. New snow covered the ramp where the ambulance was warming up. The truck's olive drab exterior disappeared against the night sky except for the red cross emblazoned on its side, floating against the white contrast behind it.

In the first of many moments of detachment that night, I wished for Hawkeye's sardonic wit or Hot Lips Houlihan's expert hands adjusting the needle in my arm. We careened down the icy autobahn at seventy-five miles an hour in an ambulance that looked like it could have seen duty in the Korean War. Every bump and sway rattled me in the stretcher, and I wondered why an ambulance, of all vehicles, didn't have shock absorbers.

These random musings would give way to concerns for John (who had not been allowed to ride with me and was probably driving like a maniac to keep up), but then I'd drift back to some arbitrary observation. The medic riding in the back with me was shivering in the cold. I could see his breath in the air, but somehow I felt enveloped in warmth. He kept switching the IV bag from one hand to the other, and at one point I think I asked him why he didn't hang it somewhere. He shrugged.

Then I noticed that his private's insignia didn't yet have the little rocker under the chevron: he had probably just gotten out of basic training and now found himself on his first medical emergency—and it wasn't at all the kind of battle wound he'd trained for. I put my own pity party aside to spare him a little.

We were an odd pair, keeping each other company on the bumpy ride. I'll be forever grateful to that young man, who was hardly more than a boy. He was the only one of the medical personnel who grasped the gravity of the situation and acknowledged, if not in words then certainly in his demeanor, that this was more than just a medical drill. The only thing he could do for me was warm the IV bag with his hands, a gesture that probably mattered less to me at the time than it did to him. It must have given him a sense of purpose, to be able to do something to comfort me. Only in retrospect was I grateful for this small act of kindness.

When we arrived at the hospital, he stood next to me until they took the bag from his hands and placed it on a hook. His parting words were more a question than a statement: "You'll be okay?"

I was. I am.

Almost thirty years later I can relive that night with a clarity reserved only for those moments that try us deeply. We all have them. I remember that I wanted very much to pray, but there was nothing more to say. I had already spent days pleading with God, striking deals, begging for the tiny life within me.

I felt abandoned.

The years have not erased those memories residing quietly in a corner of my mind. The clarity of the memories consoles me. While I may have felt abandoned on that night, hindsight reveals to me so much of God's presence, and Mary's, too, that I have to smile.

I remember that the first thing I saw when the medic wheeled me out to the ambulance was that red cross on the side of the truck. Everything else but that image had disappeared into the night. God, it seems, embraced me as they lifted me into the ambulance. If only I had recognized that then. I'm equally sure that Mary was there, keeping me calm and warm under her mantle and close to her heart even in the midst of the frozen chaos.

A Dame Who Upheld the Preciousness of Life

The most jarring part of my experience that night was how loosely the term *abortion* was thrown about. I understood that the medical term *spontaneous abortion* applied. Nevertheless, my Catholic sensibilities bristled at the word. No one present offered us condolences or acknowledged our loss. We didn't choose our situation, and yet the only kindness I remember was from a medic warming the saline.

Perhaps it is this very detachment that makes pro-life work so difficult. Until everyone involved recognizes that the dignity of the human person begins at conception and ends at natural death, a dismissive attitude that recognizes only medical procedures, not human bodies and souls, will prevail.

I raged against this injustice done to us and our unborn child for many years. The miscarriage was inevitable. The lack of compassionate care that acknowledged the loss of life was astonishingly cold: a by-product of a culture that fails to understand that life is precious at any stage, whether in utero or during suffering at the end of life.

Phyllis Bowman, the founder of the United Kingdom's Right to Life organization, understood this moral dilemma. She died a few years ago after dedicating almost half a century to the fight against abortion, embryonic experimentation (including cloning), and euthanasia.

Although Bowman founded Right to Life in 1998, she spent decades beforehand laying much of the groundwork for RTL to gain international influence. She worked in the mid-1960s to form the Society for the Protection of Unborn Children (SPUC), a lobbying group with the primary aim of putting pressure on the British Parliament in opposition to abortion, embryonic experimentation, and euthanasia. SPUC led the world in what became known as the pro-life movement. In the United States, the National Right to Life organization was founded in 1967 with a similar goal of forming legal protection for the most vulnerable in society—the unborn and infants as well as those encouraged to seek assisted suicide or euthanasia.

Bowman was an unlikely advocate for this kind of social and political pressure. In the early 1960s she was a journalist writing for the *London Evening Standard*, and she was initially in favor of the legalization of abortion. As she became more knowledgeable about the procedures and the overall impact abortion would have on society, starting with the effects on the mother, she had a change of heart. That change led her both to her work with SPUC and to the revolutionary idea that intervening with emergency funds to provide financial support to mothers so they could afford to keep their babies would save not only the children, but the mothers as well.

Bowman's journalistic gifts provided an advantage on the debate floor. Her communication skills were put to the test as she challenged parliamentary procedures and policies and made her voice known—a voice for the unborn, but also for the sick and elderly contemplating assisted suicide and euthanasia. She acknowledged that one couldn't work for the dignity of life at the early stages without recognizing the importance of life at all its stages.

I admit that a huge part of me, the part that's still outraged from that ER experience decades ago, is pleased to know that when Bowman's ire was raised, she used her verbal skills to cut deeply in defense of what she knew to be right. I'm glad to know there's more to her than a one-dimensional heroine. There's something in the power of righteous anger.

Although for much of her life Phyllis Bowman was an agnostic Jew, her work led her to convert to Catholicism; her pro-life convictions led her to embrace the gift of faith. Yet she never made religion a condition of the organizations and movements she led. To this day, both SPUC and Right to Life remain unaffiliated with any religious organization; this openness allows the movements a much wider scope.

Bowman was a formidable woman who did not give in to the opposition or allow herself or her organizations to be bullied or intimidated, even when her offices were broken into and vandalized. She merely put her staff on a rotation to remain on the premises at all times until the troubles blew over.

Threats never stopped Bowman from living her faith openly, often quoting Pope Paul VI and Pope John Paul II on matters relating to the dignity of the human person. In fact, she actively attended Church councils and conferences that promoted the understanding of the family and human life.

Pope John Paul II conferred on her the Papal Order of St. Gregory the Great, a distinction given by a pope to a layperson, man or woman, who has served the Church and society in an exceptional way. Phyllis Bowman's "battle for the baby," as she often called her advocacy, certainly qualifies as exceptional service.

In the years right before Phyllis Bowman began her advocacy for babies, another woman was fighting a similar battle, one that was very personal and ultimately cost her her life. Gianna Beretta Molla, a pregnant physician suffering from a medical emergency, denied herself the medical intervention that could have saved her life in order to protect her unborn child.

A Saint for Mothers and the Unborn

I wish I had known Gianna Beretta Molla's story years ago. I might have turned to her for solace when I felt I could no longer pray in the midst of suffering two successive miscarriages. Gianna, too, endured two miscarriages before she died after childbirth some years later.

After seeing parts of her canonization in 2004, I quickly added her to my list of saints I wanted to know better. I was drawn into her story when I discovered that her husband, Pietro Molla, and three of her children were present at her canonization. *Who was this valiant woman?*

Gianna Francesca Beretta was born in Italy in 1922, the tenth of thirteen children. Gianna grew up to be a doctor. She intended to travel to Brazil to work with her brother in the mission field, but poor health kept her in Italy. Instead, she opened her own pediatric practice and met Pietro there; they were soon married. Three children followed, and then two pregnancies that ended in miscarriage.

Gianna's last pregnancy proved to be the most difficult. She was diagnosed with a uterine fibroma that threatened her health, and doctors gave her three options: abortion, hysterectomy, or removal of only the fibroma. Although it was the most dangerous solution, Gianna opted for the removal of the fibroma midway through the pregnancy, knowing that complications would surely follow.

For Gianna, harming her unborn child was not an option. Abortion, of course, was off the table; a hysterectomy would have saved her life but would have indirectly caused her child's death. For Gianna, this was unthinkable. Gianna made it very clear that, whatever happened, no harm was to come to the baby. She delivered by caesarean section on April 21, 1962, but unfortunately a septic infection had set in due to the fibroma surgery, and Gianna died just seven days later.

In the spring of 1970, the process to promote Gianna's cause for beatification began. Her husband asked that the process be quick so as not to create too much of a disturbance with the children, particularly where their tender hearts were concerned. Remarkably, each step toward canonization did indeed move quickly, with a first miracle attributed to Gianna's intercession in 1977.

The second documented miracle God performed through her intercession was astonishing. A woman whose circumstances were similar to Gianna's in that a pressing medical condition threatened her life and her baby's life had been encouraged by her medical team to abort. The woman refused and turned herself over to Gianna's intercession. The child survived, having miraculously thrived in a womb with no amniotic fluid. The mother survived as well and was able to make a full recovery, although her extraordinarily high blood pressure had endangered her life.

If my knowledge of St. Gianna's life ended there, I'd count it as enough to adopt her as one of my patron saints. As the patron of mothers and unborn children, she's proven to be a powerful intercessor.

Defenders of Life for Modern Times

St. Gianna's heroic decision to protect her unborn child at the cost of her own life may be the defining moment in her sainthood, but her exemplary life should not be distilled into one moment. Delving further into Gianna's story shows that her entire life serves as a grand model for Christian behavior. She inspires me in a more comprehensive way.

While I'd like to think—in fact, I believe—I could lay down my life for my children, the greater challenge is whether I can accept God's will in my life *in every single moment*. St. Gianna lived her life in this manner, always a model of holiness, always a model of charity.

I look to her for guidance and hope to imitate her virtues, for in the details of St. Gianna's life I see possibilities for sanctity in my own life. She was not only a wife and mother, but also a professional. In fact, she was a working mother at the time of her death.

How did she handle the demands of her profession as a doctor and also find time to dedicate herself to her marriage and the raising of her children? I've struggled with finding that balance between my own family obligations and work. Her solution is simple to identify, but difficult to execute, especially in these modern times when the allure of being selfish with our time and resources tugs at us harder than the call to personal sacrifice. St. Gianna placed God at the center of all she did, trusting in his Divine Providence and trusting, too, in the power of prayer.

St. Gianna attended daily Mass and received Holy Communion every day after her First Holy Communion as a little girl. She prayed the Rosary daily, too, first as a young girl with her parents and then with her husband and her own children. As a professional woman, I am inspired to try to follow her example with my own family as I strive to lay down my own life for God and his will.

Phyllis Bowman fought public battles to bring the sanctity of life to the forefront of national and international attention. St. Gianna Beretta Molla fought her battle quietly and personally, a witness to her conviction until the end. Both women lived lives of heroic virtue. I aspire to do the same in my vocation.

questions to ponder

1. What does it mean to respect *human dignity*? Name a woman in your life who fits your definition. How does she exemplify respect for life at all its stages?

2. Recall a time in your life when you were called upon to serve out of respect for human dignity. What was the outcome? How did that make you feel?

3. How does your faith life reflect this respect for human dignity? Is this an area that requires further growth?

Seek moments in your interactions with others to make eye contact and acknowledge their worth.

~~~~~~

chapter six

selfless saviors
who did what
needed to be done

Irena Sendler and St. Christina the Astonishing

~~~~~~

You see a man drowning,
you must try to save him even if you cannot swim.

~Irena Sendler

I was never unhappier with my parents than the year we relocated to Miami for my father's new position at work. I was fifteen, and I didn't understand the decision they made. How they could just uproot me without a second thought as to what *I* wanted?

As a parent, I have a different perspective, especially since my husband and I made a similar decision and moved away from our close extended family to new opportunities in another state. The sacrifices my parents made and the risks they took in leaving the known for the unknown in a new industry and a new town make better sense to me now.

My parents moved us in the middle of my high school years, and I switched from a modest-sized Catholic high school to a huge, overcrowded public high school. I left a familiar group of friends I'd known since elementary school for a multicultural explosion of thousands of kids, all strangers to me. I didn't make friends right away because I was too preoccupied trying to figure out how to get to my classes in a building so full that students in the hallways moved in one-way traffic patterns. I had to figure out how to get my books without circling through a hall twice. The traffic situation was weird, but it also took me to places in the building I might otherwise not have seen and introduced me to a teacher I have never forgotten: Mr. Heilberg.

I walked past Mr. Heilberg's classroom every morning. He always stood outside his door, whistling. He whistled beautiful pieces of music, sometimes classical pieces, sometimes classic rock and roll, but always he whistled. I've never heard anyone else whistle with the same artful skill.

Years later, I returned to that high school as an English teacher and discovered that Mr. Heilberg still taught there and still stood outside his door, whistling beautifully. I recognized most of the songs, which I caught in short segments as I moved down the hall to my own classroom. Every once in a while—so rarely, in fact, that it drew my attention—Mr. Heilberg would whistle a very sad, melancholic melody.

I never asked him about his unusual talent; I just came to expect him to keep his post outside his door and whistle something from his wide repertoire of songs. In the middle of my second year of teaching at the high school, he died of a sudden illness. It was then that I learned about his remarkable life.

Mr. Heilberg had been smuggled out of Nazi-occupied Poland when he was only three years old and hidden in a convent until after World War II. His parents had perished, exterminated in the Holocaust. Somehow, extended family had been located in the United States, and he was reunited with them within a few years of being separated from his parents.

I never forgot that story. I felt a powerful connection to Mr. Heilberg that transcended our different cultures; the Polish-born Jewish man working side by side with the Cuban-born Catholic woman had more in common than I ever imagined.

Operation Pedro Pan

Mr. Heilberg died at a time when information about Operation Pedro Pan, a relocation program for Cuban refugee children in the early years of the communist regime in Cuba, was coming to the public's attention. From 1960 to 1962, more than fourteen thousand unaccompanied Cuban children were sent to the United States under the supervision of the Catholic Welfare Bureau (now Catholic Charities of the Archdiocese of Miami). Many Cuban parents sent their children to family members living in Miami in order to preserve them from Marxist-Leninist indoctrination in the government-run schools. Those without family in the United States found an opportunity through Operation Pedro Pan.

But many parents risked sending their children alone, with no family to receive them. Fear of religious persecution and retribution when Catholic schools were shut down drove these parents to make a frightening choice. They could leave their children in Cuba to be influenced by the atheist state, or they could trust the efforts of an unknown charitable organization— the Catholic Welfare Bureau was little more than a group of well-meaning and well-positioned private citizens with the heart to care for these children and find placements to keep them safe until they could be reunited with their parents.

The intent was for the children to have a safe haven until their parents could join them or recall them, but severed political ties between the United States and Cuba led to a shutdown in the program. As part of the program's design to protect parental rights, the children were placed with foster families rather than being placed for adoption, and many became adults while waiting for a reunion that never came. Many broken families remained separated permanently.

I was spared this hardship because I remained with my mother. I can't begin to imagine the anguish felt by parents who sent their children away for safety. I am astounded by the reality that this scene plays out in history time and again.

Pope John Paul II spoke about the effects of these separations during his visit to Cuba in January 1998. He recognized the "problem which has existed in Cuba for years, people being obliged to be away from the family within the country, and emigration which has torn apart whole families and caused suffering for a large part of the population."

It's a problem that continues in Cuba today. It's a problem, frankly, that exists throughout the world. Sometimes I feel insulated from these harsh realities in the world, but then I meet someone like Mr. Heilberg or encounter adults who came to the United States under the protection of Operation Pedro Pan. The information comes out in conversation if the topic of their arrival in the United States comes up.

For the most part, people offer their traumatic childhood experience as a piece of trivia in their lives, in the same way, perhaps, that I might casually say that I didn't meet my father until I was almost three.

I can't deny the effect that separation has had on my life. Today's society would label my mother a single parent during my first years, although I'm sure Mom didn't see it that way. My grandparents, aunts, and uncles played a big role in my life in those early years. My father's absence, as it turned out, was not permanent. Although it was a physical absence, it was not an emotional abandonment.

Pop, who could be quite candid and honest about most subjects, rarely spoke about this time in our lives, and then only if I pressed him. Even then, the discussion was brief, and there is much that I do not know. He tended to deflect the magnitude of his pain to ponder what my mother must have suffered during those years of separation. That was it; his pain was hers.

Nevertheless, Pop was the ultimate pragmatist and observer of the human condition. He remarked often that he and Mom, that *everyone*, did what they had to do for survival. He'd sweep his arms across an imaginary field full of people and remark with nonjudgmental emphasis that everyone rose to *their* occasion.

Some people's occasions are very private, like our experience, which has remained enclosed within the intimate layers of family until now. Others have played out publicly, open to study and scrutiny decades later.

Operation Pedro Pan received a great deal of criticism decades after the files were closed and the children had grown up. Monsignor Bryan Walsh, head of the Catholic Welfare Bureau in Miami in the early 1960s and the man behind the mass airlift of children under Operation Pedro Pan, took a huge risk when he helped create a network of men and women within Cuba to get children out of the country and to Miami. The desperation of the situation in Cuba called for an equally desperate solution. This group took risks daily even though they had no ties to the children other than a humanitarian desire to do whatever had to be done in the name of charity.

The most heroic acts seem to be called forth when the weakest and most vulnerable members of a society are endangered. The elderly, the ill, and especially children inspire in us the impulse to protect.

A Rescuer Who Chose Her Yellow Star

Twenty years before Monsignor Walsh started receiving children in Miami, a Polish woman named Irena Sendler witnessed the brutality of the Nazis who created the Warsaw ghetto, the sealed sixteen-block area where Jewish families were isolated and marked for extermination. Hundreds of thousands of Jews were channeled into this area, where they awaited their inevitable deaths.

Outraged by what she saw in the ghetto, Sendler joined the Polish resistance movement, which led to her work smuggling children out of the ghetto to safety. She was already in a position to render aid since she was a senior administrator in the Warsaw Social Welfare Department.

Sendler facilitated the registrations of many families under Christian names and then flagged their files to show they were

in quarantine with infectious diseases to protect them from
unannounced inspections. This charitable spirit was not foreign to Sendler, whose father, a doctor, often served poor Jewish
patients.

She moved in and out of the ghetto with credentials from
the Epidemic Control Department, secretly bringing food, med-
icines, and other supplies to the Jewish families. In solidarity
with the families she helped, Sendler wore the yellow star all
Jews were required to wear, although she herself was Catholic.

It was during this epidemic control assignment that she
made the decision to begin moving children out of the ghetto at
the risk of her own life. Starvation and disease were responsible
for more than five thousand deaths a month, and the children
were at greatest risk. As a young mother, she felt keenly the
desperation of these families, their distraught pleading to save
these young, innocent lives. Over the course of two years, from
1942 to 1943, Irena Sendler, with the help of confederates in the
Social Welfare Department, issued hundreds of fake identifica-
tion papers and smuggled more than 2,500 children to safety.

Unlike the thousands of children who left Cuba alone on
commercial airliners, the children Sendler smuggled out were
hidden by whatever means were available. Sometimes they were
smuggled out in burlap bags or body bags among the dead.
Other times more creative measures were taken—children were
hidden among tools or goods.

I wonder if my friend Mr. Heilberg was among the 2,500
children Irena Sendler saved during World War II. She enlisted
hundreds of families willing to shelter these children at the risk
of placing their own families in mortal danger. She had the support of the Catholic Church and sent most of the children to
convents or Church-sponsored institutions. Sendler claimed she
could always count on the sisters.

One of the things for which Mr. Heilberg was grateful was
that the sisters who took care of him maintained the integrity
of his Judaism, for his sake and in respect for his parents. I can't
help but think that he was one of those children I've read about
in these historical records.

One incredible piece of Sendler's story speaks to her understanding of the immensity of her mission. She may have been hopeful that the children would one day be reunited with their parents, but she knew the reality of the situation. The only reason these parents were willing to turn their children over to strangers was to save their lives, knowing full well their own fates. Still, Sendler kept meticulous records on all the children, documenting their real identities so that one day she could help them reunite with their families. She hid these records in glass jars that she buried.

The Gestapo eventually learned of her activities and arrested her. She was tortured, but Sendler never revealed any information that would implicate the others in her network. Her colleagues in the Polish resistance bribed her jailers, saving her from imminent execution. After the war, she returned to dig up the jars and begin the arduous task of finding the children and helping them discover their parents' fates. Tragically, most of the children's parents had been killed.

Irena Sendler, who had saved thousands of children, never relented in her efforts while there were children in need, and yet she lamented, "I could have done more. . . . This regret will follow me to my death." She sacrificed much when she saw the great need among the Jewish families in the ghetto. She put her safety and the safety of her family at stake, yet she never felt she did enough. Perhaps that's a common denominator among saints.

I, too, often feel I haven't done enough. It seems like there's always one more student to serve. I aspire to this selfless service, even if it's only in small ways with family or friends. I don't know that I have it in me to make the big sacrifices. I hope that my dad is right, though, and that I'll rise to *my* occasion.

The saints sometimes rose to *their* occasions in spectacular ways. Take, for example, St. Christina the Astonishing: she was known for flying up into trees to escape her tormentors. One legend has her flying out of a window. It makes for a good story, but the truth behind it is even more astonishing.

The Original "Flying Nun"
(and Other Astonishing Feats of Faith)

I admit that I still sometimes put the saints into neat little holy cards with one-dimensional bits of trivia. I forget they were real flesh-and-blood people very much like me, filled with hopes and desires and spiritual challenges, too.

Christina Mirabilis lived from about 1150 to 1224 in Brustem, Belgium. Her parents died when she was young, and although it is unclear how old she was when this tragedy struck, the loss of her parents must have caused practical as well as emotional difficulties for Christina.

When Christina was in her early twenties, she suffered a massive seizure that left her near death. In fact, the residual effects of the episode were so severe that she was mistaken for dead, and preparations for her funeral and burial proceeded.

She got up at her funeral, fully recovered, and astounded everyone present. I can't decide if this scene was horrifying or comical—but it certainly gave rise to the legend that she flew up into the rafters of the church. Perhaps she did, but that was only the beginning of a lifetime of miraculous events that led to her recognition as a saint in her lifetime and her subsequent designation as *Christina the Astonishing*.

With today's medical knowledge, one might suppose that Christina fell into a coma due to the stress of the seizure. Her recovery, while surprising to the witnesses who believed her to be dead, was considered a miracle.

Nevertheless, by Christina's own account, she had died. Angels had come to escort her soul to heaven and allowed her a glimpse of all the souls in torment in purgatory.

Christina couldn't bear to have witnessed their suffering without doing something for the souls in purgatory. Affirming Sendler's later observation that one cannot possibly watch a drowning man without doing something to help, Christina chose to return to earth and dedicate herself to a life of penance in reparation for the sins of the suffering souls and the conversion of sinners on earth.

The mortifications that followed were documented a few years after her death. Plunges into frozen rivers and attempted immolation in furnaces never left a mark on her. She was an outcast, often thought to be mentally ill, and was even imprisoned because of her behavior.

Part of Christina's isolation came from her unusual response to people. She claimed that the stink from sin was heavy, and she wanted to run away from it. Maybe climbing into trees to escape the stench could be seen as flying up into the trees, although I couldn't discount that she may have actually flown. Who knows? To me, what makes her astonishing is not the claim to flight or protection from physical harm but her sacrifice to atone for the sins of the souls in purgatory.

St. Christina lived a long life. It was full of turmoil and bizarre behavior that often made her an outcast. She died at the age of seventy-four from natural causes, in spite of a lifetime filled with every kind of physical test. Unlike other saints we may turn to as models of virtue, St. Christina remains an example of the bizarre and the lonely. Nevertheless, I find St. Christina heroic for delaying her entry into paradise because she saw the great need of the souls in purgatory and acted selflessly.

Why do I find her willingness to sacrifice for those in purgatory so inspiring? Purgatory isn't something a lot of Catholics talk about anymore. So reluctant are we to bad-mouth the dead that most of us would rather avoid the topic of purgatory altogether. It seems to me that St. Christina's outwardly crazy acts were the most loving and generous imaginable, for she was acting on behalf of those who could no longer help themselves—and in many cases no longer had anyone praying for them.

Seeing What Needs to Be Done

When I became a teacher, a mentor I admired gave me a little laminated card with the following story: A man was walking along a seashore strewn with starfish that had washed up on the sand and were drying out in the sun. Every few feet he would pick up a starfish and fling it back into the sea. His companion asked why he continued to strain himself in this way, since it was a useless act and he'd never save all the starfish. The man responded by picking up another starfish, saying, "It makes a difference to this one." Then he threw it back into the water.

This was an important lesson for me at the beginning of my career. I wanted to save every child I encountered. I think this is a natural response to seeing widespread need. Sometimes we don't have the resources, whether personal or institutional, to save everyone who needs saving. I think this reality might have contributed to St. Christina's distress and Irena Sendler's regret that she hadn't done more.

Sometimes I wonder if I, too, could do more.

My work is never going to be in a history book filed under acts of heroism, and that's fine with me: I'm not a professor for the accolades. But I do recognize that my work is important for each of the students I encounter. All of us are called to do our best. These two selfless women don't inspire me to go out and look for opportunities to do good. Rather, they inspire me to keep a more watchful eye within my own circles of influence to see what needs to be done there, especially with my family, friends, and people with whom I interact. Irena Sendler merely had to look outside her window to see a need. St. Christina the Astonishing acted with the same level of compassion once she became aware of a great need. I am heartened to do the same.

questions to ponder

1. Define *selflessness*. Name a woman in your life who fits your definition. How does she exemplify selfless living?
2. Recall a time in your life when you did something selfless. What was the outcome? How did that make you feel?
3. Are you being called in some way to die to self? Is there a ministry or other need that would benefit from your sacrifice of time or talent?

Think of something that needs to be done that no one else is handling. Be the hands and feet of Christ this week.

eloqvent images
of perseverance and strength

Flannery O'Connor and St. Margaret of Antioch

If you are going through hell, keep going.
~Winston S. Churchill

That's pretty sound advice. When caught in adversity's cross-hairs, you certainly don't want to stop and give up—that's the last place to be stuck. If you persevere, even enduring any necessary sacrifice, you may end up . . . well, if not in paradise, at least better off than when the journey began.

I've persevered in a few big things in my life, and I've also given up on a number of others. I persevered in my studies, earning a graduate degree while trying to be present to a husband and three small children, but I gave up guitar lessons when I was a teenager because I had trouble reading music. I don't regret the sacrifices, mine and my family's, made in the earning of that degree, but when I see my guitar leaning on its stand in the corner of my office, I am filled with longing. I regret that I didn't keep up the lessons.

That guitar is no longer a stinging reminder of failure, but rather a bit of inspiration for me to persevere in other endeavors. It's a lesson in what could have been. It reminds me that important things call for commitment, fortitude, and persistence after the initial excitement has passed.

I'm good at being excited about new projects, but not so good at staying the course once the shiny allure has faded. When things get hard and I face serious trials, I want to withdraw. I'm blessed to have a husband whose patience and example have carried me through difficult trials; he's kept me going, and we've emerged from our trials, together.

A Dragon in the Shadows

When John and I got married in the mid-1980s, it was popular in some circles for couples to write their own wedding vows. By the time John and I made the decision to get married, we had already expressed to each other in private the sentiments behind any of the vows we could have written. I mean, we'd known each other for many years. We were close friends. We were fairly certain we knew what we were getting ourselves into.

Of course, we had *no idea* what we were getting ourselves into, and that's probably a good thing. We were in love. We got married. We exchanged the traditional wedding vows: he said he'd cherish me, and I said I'd obey him. What we really should have focused on was the other part of those vows—*in sickness and in health.*

Sometime in late 2009, after almost eighteen months of uncertainty and endless testing, my husband was diagnosed with amyotrophic lateral sclerosis (ALS, or Lou Gehrig's disease). It's a progressive neurodegenerative disease that causes nerve cells in the brain and the spinal cord to deteriorate and lose their ability to control muscles in the body, leading to death. The prognosis at that time was a two- to five-year life expectancy from the onset of the disease, not necessarily from the point of diagnosis.

I've heard people say they've had the wind knocked out of them when hearing bad news. In my case, my heart was crushed by an invisible fist that barely let it beat and, sadly, barely let it feel. I walked around for a year not wanting to feel anything. Not anger, not fear, not anything.

I forgot how to pray, and I forgot, really, how to live. My ability to feel joy shriveled up, so the things that made me happy, the things that delighted me, got caught up in the same crushing hold on my heart. I squashed my desire to dream and, along with it, my ability to create anything. All my writing projects went into a box, and I never wanted to see them again.

I didn't want to be happy about anything. How could I? We had just received the most devastating news. Not only does ALS have no cure, but there is no treatment that offers any hope of recovery. It's all palliative care.

While I indulged myself in hopelessness and despair, my husband got up each morning and went to work. He continued to speak of vacation homes and travel after retirement, though I wanted him to stop. We would never have a vacation home together, and we would never travel in our retirement because he wouldn't be here with me to enjoy those things. I was committed to not enjoying anything. Ever again.

A sneaky, terrible, *insidious* creature took hold of my heart in that time. In paintings, on holy cards, in any kind of church art from sculptures to stained glass windows, the image most often used to depict the devil seems to be a dragon. I always thought it was a good metaphor—and then that dragon became real to me. I moved slowly through the stages of grief in that year, but the sense that my heart was being crushed in a vice-like grip never quite left me.

My husband, of course, is the one fighting at the front line. He is strong in many ways, not just physically. He models for me the fortitude and perseverance we both need in our lives together. John follows Churchill's advice, solidly and without bitterness, as he makes his way through this hell. He models hope for me, and that hope drives the desire to keep moving forward.

John has helped me realize that either we can shrink and allow this disease to defeat us, or we can push through the bad days and live each moment to the fullest. Some days, everything seems normal. The lawn needs to be mowed, the laundry needs to be folded and put away, and bills need to be paid. There's comfort in the mundane.

Other days he doesn't want to do anything at all because the pain from deteriorating muscles is too great. Eventually, he'll lose the ability to walk before the disease takes away all his muscle control. He still gets up to work, but that exhausts him; on those days life is hard for him, and hard for me, too. I can't kiss away this boo-boo. But it is an opportunity to love him—sometimes, by just leaving him alone; other times, by quietly sitting next to him in the dark with the soft flicker of the television casting shadows on the walls. I try not to see dragons in those shapes.

The major manifestations of the illness right now are fatigue and pain. John works straight through the pain, not giving up his promise to take care of me and our household and to provide for us in this season of our lives as we begin to wind down from our careers and settle into a slower pace.

ALS has recalibrated our lives. I could do without the illness, of course, but it has been a blessing to slow down and enjoy each other's company. Our favorite thing to do is sit outside in the roofed-in patio John built with the help of our son. We sit there for hours at a time, enjoying music he delightedly selects for me, drinking coffee, and watching the silly antics of our dog as he chases squirrels and tries to befriend deer.

Some days, we just watch the grass grow. We plan for our retirement. We look at plots for a beach house, and we debate over whether to select the prettiest beach or the beach with the best fishing. I'll let him win that argument, but not yet.

It's not easy, this unexpected turn in our lives, but it hasn't defeated us. We've slain that dragon, together, recognizing the joy in simple graces. Every morning my husband gets up for work. He comes home and cooks for us. We go to Mass on

Sunday mornings and out to dinner on Thursday nights. We persevere.

Somewhere along the way, I picked up a pen again and opened up that box full of discarded slips of paper with opening lines to poems, ideas for blog posts, and scenes for stories. I once called it the box of despair. These days, it's a box full of hope.

I've methodically catalogued the stories—and found to my surprise that I have a collection of short stories ready to share. The poems have been cleared out and published on my blog or on other websites. I'm not always successful with my follow-through, but I've looked to a faith-filled author and a dragonslayer for inspiration in the arena of perseverance.

Persevering on the Page

The return to feeling creative inspiration and being able to write was truly a gift—an outlet for my emotions and a way to explore ideas, especially in regard to my reawakened faith.

For many years, I bought into the idea that I had to be a suffering soul to write. Well, okay, maybe there is a little truth to that, now that I reflect on it, but that's not really the point I was after. I had created for myself an image of the writer as someone who lived entirely in isolation and labored under the duress of a fickle muse to produce worthy tomes of deep esoteric thought.

I don't know where I got that idea, but it has dissipated pretty quickly as I've gotten to know other writers. For the most part we can be a friendly bunch when we aren't isolating ourselves for the sake of a deadline. I've learned that writing is about hard work and perseverance. There is no muse; there is, however, discipline. Follow-through. Perseverance.

Flannery O'Connor, a Catholic writer best known for her gothic stories set in the southern part of the United States, inspires me not so much through her fiction as through her other writing. Her letters and prayer journal reveal a great deal about her writing process and spiritual life, and it is in absorbing those private thoughts of hers that I have come to an understanding of my own process. She famously said that she needed to write to discover what she thought; I find myself writing paragraphs and paragraphs before I get around to making my point. It takes work to do this: first to get the thoughts on paper, and then to clean them up so they follow some kind of logical path. To know that a writer of O'Connor's caliber worked hard at perfecting her craft encourages me immensely.

As an English teacher, I can always count on at least one of her short stories being available in an anthology. My favorite is "A Good Man Is Hard to Find." The grandmother's over-the-top behavior and outrageous statements lead me to feel a little sympathy toward The Misfit, even though he is the sociopathic killer.

O'Connor wrote about the human condition. I enjoy teaching about the quirky characters, but I especially love the wonderful discussions with my students that follow those readings. Critics often refer to her stories, and especially her characters, as grotesque. I don't disagree with that label, although I prefer to say that she captures the raw, exposed reality of humanity. She explores the workings of grace in the worlds she creates. No doubt it is the same grace she found in her own life.

She captures this human angst in her stories, but I especially love her personal correspondence. She also published more than one hundred book reviews in the mid-1900s in the *Georgia Bulletin* and *The Southern Cross*, two Catholic newspapers in Georgia. In them, she explored topics in theology and doctrine that continue to resonate today. I wonder how she might have embraced social media, with blogging accessible to everyone. O'Connor's style in those book reviews, provocative and thoughtful, is echoed today by any number of popular Catholic writers and bloggers. It is part of what inspires me today in my own blog.

O'Connor was a fascinating woman; she persevered in her gifted writing through much suffering. She developed a devastating illness, systemic lupus erythematosus, and died when she was just thirty-nine years old. I feel empathy for her, but also look to her strength and perseverance for a model in overcoming adversity. As lupus has many similarities with ALS, I'm drawn to O'Connor to better understand my husband, as well as myself.

John and I struggle together and apart, persevering in living a life as close as possible to normal while accepting the limitations imposed upon us by illness, something O'Connor did with finesse. She seems to have been destined for literary greatness. In addition to studying at the prestigious Iowa Writers' Workshop and earning an MFA from the University of Iowa, she won numerous awards and grants. She was just beginning her literary career when she was diagnosed. The lupus proved to be debilitating, so she returned home to Milledgeville, Georgia, where she lived with her mother and continued writing steadily for the remainder of her life.

As her health declined, she wrote novels and short stories and book reviews; she went on speaking tours and had a robust correspondence; on top of all that, she found time to raise more than one hundred peafowl. It delights me to know she found joy in nature. That, and the thought she might have been chased by a peacock or two.

I'd like to emulate O'Connor's work ethic. She maintained a daily routine of writing for three hours in the morning. I can't wrap my mind around this kind of discipline, since I tend to write in little spurts and sprints of a hundred words here and there. But O'Connor created this schedule early in her writing days at the Writers' Workshop and maintained it throughout her life. I was surprised, and a little consoled, to learn that some days she would stare at a blank page for those three hours. But she maintained the routine, and it is that persistence that I admire.

Defeating the Dragon

O'Connor often revealed the action of God's grace in her short stories, but she exhibited a great deal more grace in her own life. Her struggle with lupus may have ended in her untimely death, but it was no defeat. In her book *Mystery and Manners*, she wrote:

> St. Cyril of Jerusalem, in instructing catechumens, wrote: "The dragon sits by the side of the road, watching those who pass. Beware lest he devour you. We go to the Father of Souls, but it is necessary to pass by the dragon." No matter what form the dragon may take, it is of this mysterious passage past him, or into his jaws, that stories of any depth will always be concerned to tell, and this being the case, it

> requires considerable courage at any time, in any country,
> not to turn away from the storyteller (p. 35).

The imagery of a dragon waiting to pounce on and devour the traveler speaks to me at the visceral level. I still don't want to think about the trials I'll face in the coming years—disability, death, and loneliness; however, projecting those threats as a dragon, while frightening, is also a great consolation. That image of the evil one who presents himself when we face hardships and crouches by, ready to devour our hope and resolve, is repeatedly defeated by St. Margaret of Antioch. This inspires me to no end.

I love that St. Margaret of Antioch is often depicted with a slain dragon at her feet. We know very little about her beyond the legends that surround her. She's one of those saints I am drawn to, not because I know her virtues up front, but because the images of her have an emotional appeal that attracts me.

I want a saint who can slay dragons.

I need that strength.

St. Margaret was a virgin and martyr in the third century, the daughter of a pagan priest. Upon the death of her mother, she was put in the charge of a Christian nurse, who raised young Margaret as a Christian. She disappointed her father by refusing to give up her love of Christ, although she suffered much as her father tried to change her mind.

Eventually, she drew the attention of one of the city's prefects, Olybrius, who served under Emperor Diocletian and took part in his persecution of Christians. Margaret turned Olybrius down, and in retribution he had her imprisoned, scourged, tortured with irons, and stretched on the rack.

Perhaps this perseverance through trials gave rise to the legend that surrounds St. Margaret. While she was imprisoned, the story goes, the devil appeared to her in the guise of a dragon. When she refused to be frightened into submission, he devoured her. She had a crucifix in her hand, which irritated his stomach, and so the dragon regurgitated her unharmed. He got what he deserved—did he think he could consume Christ? St. Margaret held on to her beliefs and couldn't be defeated. She prayed constantly during her trials, believing prayer delivered her. I love the legend, but the truth behind it inspires me equally and provides me with true recourse when facing trials: St. Margaret most likely crossed herself and in that action dispelled the images taunting her.

Living in Gratitude and Trust

Margaret persevered in prayer, thanking God at every new trial that she did not surrender her faith. It resonates powerfully with me that St. Margaret's prayer was in thanksgiving rather than supplication, even though the horrendous trials she faced would ultimately lead to her martyrdom. Finding something to be grateful for in the midst of her trials must have given her the strength to withstand the temptation to renounce her faith. Flannery O'Connor wrote often about gratitude—gratitude for her father, who died young of the same disease that plagued her; gratitude for the inspiration she received from God; and gratitude, finally, for the grace in finding meaning in her affliction with lupus.

I understand that so well, as John and I have grown to see the precious gift of every day; how joyfully we express gratitude for even the simplest thing, like unexpected birdsong or a cool breeze. My husband, whose sweet faith was inspired by his grandmother, reminds me often that God will always take care of us. We must trust him and look to him in all things.

I admit it's a difficult thing to do, to let go of my control and trust in his goodness. It was especially difficult when my broken heart was constricted and hardened against everything. To protect myself from the pain of my grief, I shut out everything, including Jesus. I hadn't completely given up, but I was close.

Jesus, however, is abundantly merciful, and he is the perfect model of perseverance. While I may have given up on him, he never abandoned me; he found a different way into my heart. He showed me a heart just as broken as mine, his Sacred Heart so illuminated with his love that his hands had to hold it together to keep it from bursting—the exact opposite of my own heart in its tight grip of fear and despair. He persevered in drawing me back to him, and I am forever grateful.

We can't anticipate what sort of dragons lie in wait for us, but we can be consoled with the truth that if we persevere in our prayer, our faith, our gratitude, and our trust in the Lord, in the end we will emerge victorious.

questions to ponder

1. Define *perseverance*. Name a woman in your life who fits your definition. What dragon did she face, and did she defeat it?
2. Recall a time in your life when you persevered. What was the outcome? Did you slay your dragon? How did that make you feel?
3. Where in your spiritual life do you need perseverance? Have you taken on a new devotion or discipline? Are you struggling with making a change?

Ask a saint to pray for you as you persevere through your trials.

passionate beauties who made the world a better place

Audrey Hepburn and St. Rose of Lima

The beauty of a woman is seen in her eyes, because that is the doorway to her heart, the place where love resides.

~Audrey Hepburn

When the Columbia Pictures logo with the image of that majestic woman standing on the pedestal flashes on the movie screen, everyone in my family cheers a little bit.

"Columbia" looks just like Mom.

My mother is one of the most beautiful women I know. My father had a photograph of her as a very young woman, maybe in her late teens or early twenties, that rivaled any of the

Hollywood beauties of the fifties and sixties. Big brown eyes rimmed with long dark lashes and the fashionable thick eyebrows from that era gave her a deep, mysterious countenance, but her smile softened the look—she was warm, not sultry.

It is still my favorite picture of her and is how my heart continues to see her.

A lot of people say I look like my mother. I'll take the compliment, but in truth I look more like my father and his mother. My sister is the one who got Mom's looks. I'm okay with that: I got a lot from Mom. My curly hair is the same dark shade as hers, only thick and unruly. My eyes are dark, too, and I suffered with my thick brows in an era when pencil thin was in, but I'm happy for it now.

I know that I resemble her enough for people to guess I'm her daughter. Even so, I never really thought I was beautiful. I was the awkward kid who always seemed to be marching along to a different drummer. I didn't quite look like the other girls—they were all blonde or had light brown hair, except for the occasional redhead. And then there was me. I didn't look like our dolls or like the little girls in the storybooks.

When the other girls were running off to ballet lessons, I was sweating in the gym playing basketball. While they practiced flirting with the boys, I hid behind my glasses and stuck my nose in my books. I felt a bit like the ugly duckling, not quite fitting in. I matured physically rather quickly, which created a new set of problems—mostly for my parents; I was happy for the new-found attention from boys. And yet I also bought into the notion that beauty was external; therefore, I never quite accepted that I was beautiful, too. I had some growing up to do before I understood the depth of real beauty.

The Beauty of Unconditional Love

After thirty years together, my husband still tells me I'm beautiful; I smile and reciprocate with a kiss. I used to dismiss his compliments. They often came at the end of the day when the hair I had so carefully tamed in the morning had been pulled back into a ponytail, a halo of frizz sprouting along my hairline.

More than once when he said this to me, I was wearing the same T-shirt in which I had fallen asleep the night before, standing amid the chaos of little ones clamoring for attention as I tried to get dinner ready. And yet, my husband found me . . . beautiful.

John has always preferred me in jeans and a ponytail, without makeup and without primping. I misunderstood this for many years, thinking he was trying to keep some youthful image of me alive. I eventually came to understand that the beauty he saw was in my attitude and in my service to him and our family. If I was comfortable, I was free to be me. He saw, and made me realize, that my face radiates joy and love when I am doing something for him and our children. There is great beauty in the expression of love.

When my children were infants, I loved holding them close to me and bringing their faces up to mine. I was always searching for that special moment when we would make eye contact, which elicited a spontaneous smile from the little one. Often, the children would reach up to touch my face and we would enjoy a snuggle and a little laughter. In the sweet tenderness of those moments, I'd think of how the infant Jesus must have lovingly touched Mary's face as she held him close to her bosom. It brings to mind, too, the tenderness with which she must have held him and stroked his face one last time when they brought him down from the Cross and laid him in her lap.

Motherhood introduced me to unconditional love. I never understood God's love for us until I had children of my own. Not everyone comes to this understanding in the same way; I am grateful to have been blessed to experience it through motherhood.

Self-sacrifice and living for others doesn't come naturally. It calls for living outside ourselves and putting others first. I can say that as a young mother I would have preferred many nights to roll over in bed and go back to sleep rather than get up for a feeding. Sleep still looked better years later when I was waiting up for older teens to get home. In between were many years of sacrifice.

Today my children are grown and the worries have changed, but the sacrifice continues in other forms. It seems as though I spent the first part of my motherhood on my knees dressing my children and playing with them. Now I'm on my knees praying for them! I think the first part was training for the intensity of this second part, where I find myself more often than not at the foot of the cross. The empty nest brings new worries, not about broken bones, but about broken hearts, not about growing pains, but about career moves and relocations.

I'll admit that on more than one occasion I have escaped into a good book or late-night movie classic to imagine, for a while, a different life. But then I happily return to my reality. My life is where my loves are. My husband. My children. My extended family and friends. It may be gritty sometimes, and other times colossally boring, but it is *my* life. And it is beautiful. *I* am beautiful, whether I'm wearing pearls or doing the dishes—some days, both.

Living Deep Beauty

One of my favorite actresses, Audrey Hepburn, radiates beauty unlike any other woman I have ever known.

Many people associate Hepburn with the character Holly Golightly from one of her best-known films, *Breakfast at Tiffany's*—in the iconic "little black dress" with white gloves, her hair swept up into a high bun, wearing diamonds and wielding a cigarette holder like a magic wand. She is stunning. Gorgeous. Flawless. And yes, superficial.

But Audrey Hepburn the actress was much more than superficially beautiful. Throughout her life she radiated confidence and serenity. She played a number of interesting characters in her stage and film career, but her personal life, especially as a youth, was far more intriguing than the fictional lives she portrayed on the screen.

Although she was born in Belgium and was a British citizen, she had familial ties to the Netherlands through her mother's family. She spent much of her childhood traveling throughout the three countries. During World War II, Hepburn went into hiding after the German occupation of the Netherlands. When she was about fourteen years old, one of her brothers was captured and sentenced to a Nazi labor camp, the other went into hiding to avoid a similar fate, and her uncle was executed after being implicated in sabotage with the Dutch resistance movement.

Having studied ballet since she was five, Hepburn was an accomplished dancer, and during the war she put on several performances to raise money for the Dutch resistance. She famously noted that these performances ended solemnly, with no applause. Offstage, the heroic young woman served as a courier for the Dutch resistance, delivering secret packages during the war. She witnessed many of the horrors of this time.

When Allied forces liberated the Netherlands, a United Nations relief delegation found her malnourished and suffering from several physical ailments, including anemia. She said she had seen much in the war, as a mere child watching other children, particularly Jews, transported by train to places unknown to her, and it left a deep mark.

Many years later, about the time her film career was slowing down and she was spending less time in the studio, Audrey Hepburn became an ambassador for the United Nations, the same organization that rescued her as a child during the war. She dedicated the last years of her life, before succumbing to cancer at age sixty-one, to extensive travel in Africa, Asia, and South America, where she brought attention to the plight of children affected by war, famine, and extreme poverty.

At first it seemed a little out of place for a Hollywood starlet to disappear from the limelight. A beautiful woman should be the center of attention. Yet she demurred when too much attention was placed on her looks. "True beauty in a woman is reflected in her soul. It is the caring that she lovingly gives, the passion that she shows. . . ."

The most beautiful pictures of Audrey Hepburn don't show her in diamonds and Givenchy dresses. Instead, she is crowded by smiling children clamoring to be held by her or carried on her back, and she welcomes it. You can see it in her smile. She is still stunning. Still gorgeous. Still flawless. And full of unspoken passion.

A Beautiful Rose

St. Rose of Lima shared a vision with Audrey Hepburn for helping the poor and sick even though they lived almost four hundred years apart. Like Hepburn, Rose was very beautiful and very committed to helping the poor. Unlike Hepburn, who had no formal religious leanings, St. Rose committed herself to Christ as a very young woman, much to her parents' displeasure.

St. Rose was born in Lima, Peru, in April 1586. Her real name was Isabel, but she was so beautiful that she was called Rose; the name stuck. Her widely admired beauty became such a problem for her that she would rub pepper on her face to make it blotchy and unattractive. St. Rose didn't want any deterrents to her plan to be a bride of Christ.

She wanted to consecrate her life to a religious vocation, but her parents wanted her to marry. She refused, and after ten years of disappointment, her father gave in and let her have a room of her own in their home. She became a member of the Third Order of St. Dominic since she was denied permission to enter the convent.

St. Rose was obedient, and she was also a dutiful and humble daughter. When her parents fell into financial ruin, St. Rose redoubled her efforts by working in the home during the day and sewing at night. Her life was filled with loneliness, but she would often pray, asking the Lord to increase her suffering as a way to also increase her love for him. St. Rose was known to wear a silver crown that had spikes along the inner edges to remind her of Christ's suffering in his Passion. These mortifications did little to suppress her beauty because her beauty emanated from within. When she spoke of Jesus, her face became beatific. Her skin glowed; her eyes sparkled. The love in her heart illuminated her face.

St. Rose could have lived a holy life in the quiet obscurity of her bedroom. Instead, she lived a life of service, turning her room into a place where she could care for the homeless children in her community. She also took care of the sick and the elderly until she died of illness at the age of thirty-one.

Audrey Hepburn and St. Rose of Lima, beautiful according to society's standards, demonstrated a purer beauty that came from the heart. Their loving service became the true measure of their beauty.

Beauty Is in Caring

My mother doesn't look like that picture my father kept on his dresser anymore. More than fifty years have passed since it was taken, and a lifetime of experience has altered her. Her hair is thinner. Her smile is still warm, but her eyes show the passage of time—they aren't as clear as they used to be, and fine lines serve as records of her laughter and tears. Her beauty, however, surpasses the image caught on film so many years ago. It is real flesh-and-blood beauty, the kind that manifests itself in action. In love.

Every morning, for as long as I can remember, my mother has gotten up at dawn and made coffee. Two kinds of coffee: espresso for a little morning jolt, and drip to enjoy and savor over breakfast and conversation with my father as they went about their morning routine.

I imagine she still gets up at dawn and makes coffee, but now it's for one. My father passed away this year. To say it was a difficult year diminishes the impact his death has had on all of us, on my mother most of all. Demanding. Punishing. Wearisome. These are words that begin to describe the experience.

My father suffered immense pain from the cancer that ravaged his body, and my mother suffered twice: once beside him, and then again alone. It was a tragic dance, a choreography of missteps and missed steps, but equally graceful and filled with grace. I wouldn't wish this dance on anyone, of course, but as usual my parents managed to teach us a remarkable lesson through their loving example. There was pain, to be sure, but there was also joy. And something else.

At first I thought it was resignation or maybe acceptance. I'm sure it was a little of both, but there was still something more. Fortitude. Both my father *and* my mother bore this illness with courage and endurance. It wasn't just a matter of facing daily setbacks, but facing them, letting them pass, and getting up the next day to do it again. I saw my mother's love in action: Standing and helping with a two-hour morning routine that used to take fifteen minutes. Preparing a full place setting for each of eight small meals that were never fully consumed. Sitting quietly for hours for the company and the presence and nothing more, because that was everything.

My mother became more beautiful by the moment, radiating love in every action. Many people prayed for my parents, for all of us, this past year. It's nice to know people pray for you, but it's truly amazing to see how it manifests itself right in front of you. Galatians 5:22–23 tells us that "the fruit of the Spirit is love, joy, peace, patience, kindness, generosity, faithfulness, gentleness, and self-control." The Holy Spirit was clearly present in my parents' home, accompanying them on this last journey.

This was loving service at its best. Audrey Hepburn made a profound difference, not just in the lives of the individuals she touched, but in changing a mind-set and creating a vehicle for others to do the same. There is much to be admired in her work and, today, in the work that others such as Angelina Jolie continue. But how much more potent is the beauty of that loving service when it is done in the name of Christ! St. Rose didn't have the reach of a wealthy celebrity, but she had the burning love of Jesus in her heart. No amount of suffering could extinguish that.

Audrey Hepburn's assertion that a woman's beauty is in the care she lovingly gives inspires me. It reminds me of my mother.

questions to ponder

1. Define *beauty*. Name a woman in your life who fits your definition. How does she exemplify inner beauty in a world preoccupied with superficial beauty?
2. What makes you beautiful? List those qualities. Embrace them.

3. How can your inner beauty inspire others? Do you serve
    with a smile? Do you love others, even when it is difficult?

*Thank Jesus for those qualities that make you beautiful. Offer them to
the Blessed Virgin Mary and ask her to magnify them in you in the
service of her Son.*

~~~~~~

chapter nine

Compassionate souls who helped the hopeless and suffering

Dorothea Lange and Bl. Rosalie Rendu

~~~~~~

Let us love the Good God very much. Let us not be sparing
with our duty; let us serve the poor well,
always speaking to them with great kindness. . . .
Our Lord hides behind those rags.

~Bl. Rosalie Rendu

I knew Dorothea Lange's photography decades before I knew
her name. I first saw her portrait *Migrant Mother* as we zipped
through the chapter on the Great Depression in middle school.
I would see the photo again in books and articles about poverty

and occasionally in journalism books because of its status as an iconic representation of an era.

When I was in college I wrote for the student newspaper, but I didn't last very long as a journalist: I was too nonconfrontational to get in anyone's face demanding answers. I love photography and am drawn to the pathos in photographs like Lange's, but I've always felt that taking a picture of someone's pain is a violation of his or her privacy. I've tried a time or two, and even succeeded in getting good pictures, but afterward I felt I had been intrusive.

Although my feelings about taking the pictures myself inhibit me, I do admire the results when others take phenomenal pictures of the human condition—all of it, from beautiful candid moments of joyful scenes to the wretched effects of poverty, loneliness, and even despair.

The Lens Captures a Story

I am a storyteller, and I think some of the best stories are captured in photographs. That's why *Migrant Mother* touched me as a young teen and why it continues to elicit from me a wave of compassion, even though the woman pictured has long passed on and her children probably have, too. I admire Dorothea Lange's courage to tell this story of poverty and bring it to the attention of the nation.

The migrant woman's eyes seem to take her out of the picture even though she is surrounded by her children. They hide their faces, perhaps from the photographer's scrutiny. Part of the fascination of the picture is in the woman's faraway look and her hand placed absentmindedly on her face. Worry etches that face.

I've seen that expression dozens of times on the faces of others. That look makes me uncomfortable every time, although I can't always identify exactly why. Is it the silent evidence of poverty? Suffering? Hopelessness? The realization that but for the grace of God, it could be me.

Dorothea Lange didn't begin her career as a photojournalist. She studied photography as an art form at Columbia University in the 1920s and specialized in portrait photography. Her studies led to a career as a portrait photographer with her own successful studio in San Francisco.

This might have been where her story ended, except that she started photographing the unemployed men who stood in breadlines during the Great Depression. She often included captions that were the actual words of her subjects, adding a deeper layer to the impact of the photographs. I respect this approach; Lange honored the men's stories by encouraging them to tell them.

Eventually, Lange left her lucrative business and entered into documentary photography by capturing images of Native Americans in the Southwest. Soon she was documenting the effects of poverty on migrant farmworkers for the Farm Security Administration, a new branch of the US Department of Agriculture. Because she was working for the federal government, Lange never made any money on the sale of these photographs.

I most appreciate that she captured the heart of the pain and suffering of these Americans without crossing the line into exploitation. According to her partner, Lange would retire her camera if she saw in her subjects the slightest sign of discomfort or objection to being photographed. She waited to establish a relationship, if not of trust, then at least of nonconfrontation. She viewed the camera lens as a tool for justice and was often disappointed when her work did not achieve the change she hoped for.

Seeing through My Own Lens

My first teaching job, in the Little Havana neighborhood of Miami, introduced me to people who were in situations similar to the ones Lange photographed and documented. In the 1980s in Miami, immigrants came primarily from two areas in the Caribbean: Cuba and Haiti.

Perhaps my eyes had already been primed by the image of *Migrant Mother* to recognize the look I saw on the faces of the clients I served. The people I taught were gaunt, big-eyed, quiet. It was their silence that spoke to me the loudest. I never knew whether it was pride or resignation. They just accepted what

~~~~~~

chapter ten

resolute seekers of peace and reconciliation

Immaculée Ilibagiza and St. Rita of Cascia

~~~~~~

Each of us has a mission on earth. It is simply a
question of seeking how God can use us to make
His Gospel known and lived.

~St. Marie Eugénie Milleret

In the spring of 1994, I was blissfully occupied with my young
family. My children were ages two, four, and six, and my world
revolved around them and my husband. Those years were spent
shuttling little people to parks, beaches, and, most afternoons,
to their grandparents' house on the corner. Impromptu "tea"
parties in the shade of the carport, with juice boxes and Goldfish
crackers, delighted all of us.

We enjoyed a happy relationship with our neighbors, so
often there were extra little ones at the kids' multicolored picnic

table, and I had the opportunity to talk with adults about something other than purple dinosaurs. Those peaceful afternoons were lovely breaks from my harried week of school, laundry (always laundry!), and other household chores.

On the other side of the world, neighbors were killing neighbors in a horrific massacre that came to be known as the Rwandan Genocide. Decades of political unrest coupled with serious conflict between the two main ethnic groups in Rwanda, the Tutsi and the Hutu peoples, led to an uprising by extremist nationalist Hutus to murder the minority Tutsis. Radio and television broadcasts encouraged Hutu citizens to kill their Tutsi neighbors, and the killing increased to frenzied levels in many parts of the country. Within three months, almost one million people were murdered.

My Cousin Lives Her Calling

I was oblivious to this news, busy with my own concerns. I became aware of the genocide only when requests came from family to pray for one of my Basque cousins. Sr. Mercedes, or Mertxe as she is known in the family, was going to Rwanda, where the sisters of her order had schools, in order to assist in the country's recovery. We were stunned—both at the horror of the massacre and at the news that Mertxe had volunteered to go.

Mertxe's order, the Religious of the Assumption, was founded in Paris by St. Marie Eugénie Milleret and is dedicated to prayer and education. Transforming society is at the heart of their work; their vision of education is that it frees the human person to transform society through love. The sisters' joyful work in community leads to the formation of many deep friendships with women of diverse backgrounds. Congregations of the Religious of the Assumption are found throughout Europe, Africa, Asia, North and South America, and the Caribbean.

The Religious of the Assumption operates schools in Rwanda, and Mertxe had friends there. In April 1994, when the massacre began, there were 102 sisters in Rwanda operating ten schools and two medical dispensaries. About half of the sisters identified as Hutu, and the other half, Tutsi. Six of the sisters were murdered, among them Mertxe's dear friend Sr. Bonny (Bonifacia). The remaining sisters fled with thousands of their students to Goma, in what is now the Democratic Republic of the Congo.

Mertxe, mourning over the genocide and still trembling over the news of Sr. Bonny's death, heard that Caritas International had requested aid from European institutions. She responded to the call immediately, moved by the memory of Sr. Bonny, a humble, wise, and strong woman—a woman of God. Mertxe knew that had circumstances been reversed, Sr. Bonny would have sprung into action on a mission of peace, forgiveness, and reconciliation.

Mertxe called the mother general in Paris to obtain permission to go to Rwanda and was given 100 percent support from the congregation. Within ten days, on June 24, 1994, the Feast of St. John the Baptist, she left her hometown of Telleriarte, Spain, after praying at the Shrine of St. John the Baptist, where she had made her perpetual vows some twenty years earlier. She arrived in Paris for an orientation to fortify her physically, psychologically, morally, and spiritually for the work ahead. She was afraid, and yet she prayed for strength, that like the Baptist she would prepare the way for those who needed to hear the gospel. Later, Mertxe would laugh and admit she didn't want to have St. John the Baptist's luck and lose her head.

We laughed with her. But we knew it wasn't an unfounded fear. The cargo plane that took them to Cameroon was filled with humanitarian aid: bags of rice, corn, beans, and other items. Their hearts were filled with love. The Caritas team was then transported to a camp near Goma, on Lake Kivu, where they joined the sisters who were already there working for peace and reconciliation.

Lake Kivu had been one of the most beautiful places in Rwanda. When the team arrived, it was gruesome—hundreds of bodies were floating in the lake. Immediately Merxte's team had to put into action all the training they had received in Paris. That lake was the people's source of water. They bathed there.

They took water for drinking from it. The temperatures were high . . . and thirst unquenchable.

The nauseating smell of death hung in the air, and for the first days they were hardly able to work because of the stench. The volunteers who had arrived before them had been unable to keep up with the seemingly endless need to dig trenches for burial. More than eight hundred thousand refugees from Rwanda had congregated in Goma. Mertxe's task, with the other sisters of her order who were there, was to care for five thousand children. The majority of them were from the schools operated by the Religious of the Assumption.

The sisters' work with the children, from sunup to sundown, was exhausting. Mertxe's charge was a group of fifty children aged six to eight. The instructions given to her were simple: care for them and mother them. Love them. All of the children were orphans. She still sees their faces, hears their cries for *Mama! Papa!*

Within this tragic scene Mertxe discovered a deep capacity for love that she had never known. She says, "The children taught me to *look upon others* with tenderness. To *listen* with tenderness. To *love* with tenderness. To *caress* with tenderness. And the Lord of tenderness was there with us, in the midst of our pain."

At night the adults on her team (four Rwandan sisters, two from Burkina Faso, one from France, three from Spain [including Mertxe]; and four lay teachers from Rwanda) would retire and pray by candlelight. They offered each other support. They cried together. They encouraged each other. And most of all, they experienced God's love among them. His presence was felt deeply as they grew in faith, hope, and love. Merxte lived fully in each moment, as God permitted and circumstances dictated. Mertxe's mission witnessed to the reality that people from different cultures and different mind-sets can coexist peacefully. They were an example of faith in action, planting seeds of hope.

An estimated one million people perished during that terrible span of three months. Those who survived live with horrific consequences; Rwanda is a country still in recovery, not just politically and economically, but on a very personal level. One of those survivors, a young Tutsi woman named Immaculée Ilibagiza, spoke at a Eucharistic Congress I attended in Atlanta, Georgia, some years ago. Her story demonstrates how faith, when put into action, can inspire great changes, both in individuals and in communities.

Grace That Cannot Hide

The first thing you notice about Immaculée is her smile. It radiates from within her with such joyful intensity that you'd never believe for a moment that it could be generated by someone who has suffered what she has at the hands of her fellow man. Her parents and two of her three beloved brothers were murdered in the genocide. She was spared by hiding in a three-by-four-foot bathroom with seven other women. The pastor who hid them from his family and the authorities was not always sympathetic to them, yet he felt compelled to protect them.

Immaculée had come home from college for Easter that April to find her family in distress over events in their community. The Hutu president's plane had been shot down, escalating tensions between the Hutu and Tutsi peoples, and one of her brothers was begging that the family leave and make their way into Zaire. He had heard rumors that a killing squad had formed and that their family was on the list of targets.

Because Immaculée's family lived close to the shore of Lake Kivu, an escape would have been easy at that moment. The couple of days they waited proved the rumors to be true and made a clean escape impossible. In the midst of angry mobs wielding machetes, murdering people right before their eyes, Immaculée's father sent her away to ask for protection at a pastor's home in town.

Immaculée gave her father a scapular she had worn while away at college, urging him to wear it. They both understood that he would very likely die in the carnage, but he tried to comfort her, giving her his rosary and telling her to keep praying. When she arrived at the pastor's house, she was met with a cold reception. The pastor allowed her to stay for the night, along with her brother and a friend who had escorted her, but it became clear to Immaculée that their welcome would be short-lived.

News of the continuing massacre disturbed everyone, including the pastor, a Hutu fearful of being implicated as a Tutsi sympathizer. The situation escalated quickly, and Immaculée found herself rushed to say her good-byes to her brother, who was evicted from the pastor's home. Then the pastor secretly took Immaculée and five other women to his private rooms, where he deposited them in the bathroom with a warning that they must not make a sound.

The women complied, fearful for their lives and grateful for this mercy. Soon, the sounds of angry raiders filled the grounds and house. The women could hear the conversations of their hunters. They remained in those close quarters for one hundred days, fearing for their lives every moment. Toward the end of their ordeal, two other women were added to the already impossibly cramped bathroom, and yet they survived.

Although the pastor would bring them water and food as he was able, it was difficult for him to procure food without calling attention to the fact he was hiding Tutsis in the house. One time, the women were almost discovered when he relaxed his guard for a moment and let them leave the bathroom in order to watch a movie. The light from the television alerted a servant, who turned him in to the Hutu extremists, resulting in another intense search of the premises.

Immaculée prayed and prayed. She filled those first days with prayers to be spared the horrors that awaited her outside that bathroom door. Other days, she became so frightened that she couldn't pray. Sometimes anger and rage consumed her, and she entertained thoughts of killing the aggressors. She struggled constantly with the voices in her head, sure that the evil one taunted her with despair.

Immaculée could often feel her heart filling with hatred, even though she didn't want to fall prey to those thoughts. She tried to pray for the extremists, but found she couldn't. Finally, she prayed differently, asking that Jesus open her heart so she could forgive.

God spoke to her then, in the depth of her need, reassuring her that they are *all* his children, the Tutsi and the Hutu alike. He asked her to forgive her persecutors, and she immediately found it possible to pray for the Hutu extremists. She prayed unceasingly after that. Prayer, she said, was her armor. That bathroom prison became an unexpected blessing for her. It is where she found God and where he filled her heart with love and forgiveness.

St. Teresa of Avila said that "joy is not the absence of suffering, but *the presence of God.*" What else could explain Immaculée's joyful smile?

The situation in the pastor's home became more difficult. Extended family joined him, fleeing violence in the northern part of the country. After three months of close calls, the pastor and the women were convinced that luck was running out. One more intense search of the house would reveal the hidden women, and that would mean certain death for all of them.

In the early hours of the morning, the women were marched out of the house with an armed escort made up of the pastor and his nephew, Immaculée's former boyfriend. They headed toward a camp established by French soldiers who had been sent as part of a humanitarian mission. The frightened group marched past a small group of machete-armed militants, but they felt emboldened to continue until they faced a larger group. At that point, the men, fearing for their own lives, left the women to their own devices to cross the final five hundred yards to safety.

Immaculée stared down the militants and summoned the strength to get all the women to the French camp, where they were taken for spies. Thanks to a series of events that Immaculée believes was God's hand moving among them, a soldier in the camp recognized her and vouched for her credibility.

Immaculée had found peace with God through prayer during her ordeal in hiding. She had also found peace with the Hutu mobs who had destroyed everything and everyone she loved. She forgave her family's murderers, finding room in her heart to pity them and pray that they would have a change of heart, for their own sakes.

While she was in the French camp, one of the officers, sympathetic to her suffering, offered to take revenge for her. She had only to give him the names of her family's killers and he would take care of executing them. She refused, to the man's surprise.

Later, when Immaculée had physically recovered and was working for the United Nations, she took the opportunity to go back to her home in the hope of finding some closure. She was able to bury the remains of one of her brothers and of their mother. Then she did the most heroic thing of all. She visited the man who killed them. He had been convicted of war crimes and was being held locally. Immaculée had the man brought to her so she could look him in the eyes. He avoided making eye contact, but she persisted until he did; then she spoke the words aloud to him: "I forgive you."

Could you have done such a thing? Can you imagine finding the strength to look your own parents' killer in the eye and pronounce a benediction of grace? This extraordinary act of forgiveness and reconciliation seems humanly impossible. And yet, God calls us just the same . . . has always called his children to do the impossible—with the strength he gives them.

A Holy Peacemaker

St. Rita of Cascia was born in 1381 in Roccaporena, Italy. Most people may know her as the patron saint of abused wives or difficult marriages, but she shares another patronage with the more popular St. Jude: she is also the patron of impossible causes. This patronage has as its basis the miraculous turnaround she accomplished in her community after her husband was killed in a long-standing feud. St. Rita brought reconciliation to a town in desperate need of peace.

When Rita was twelve years old, her parents arranged a marriage to Paolo Mancini, a rich and powerful man in Cascia, even though Rita had wanted to join a convent. He proved to be an abusive husband, guilty of verbal and physical abuse and successive infidelities. His immoral behavior was widespread in the region, and he had many enemies as a result. Inevitably, a serious feud developed with another family in Cascia.

Rita had two sons with Paolo, and she lived in fear not only of his abuse, but also of what her sons would become given the environment in which they were being raised. She prayed fervently for Paolo's conversion for many years and raised their sons in the Christian faith. Rita met her husband's abuse with kindness and humility, eventually converting him, if not completely to Christianity, at least to giving up his abusive behavior. She also succeeded in convincing him to give up the bitter feud. Unfortunately, the other family held on to the animosity, and one of its members stabbed Paolo to death.

Paolo's brother, intent on seeking revenge, encouraged Rita's sons, now young men, to join him. Even though Rita publicly forgave her husband's murderer at his funeral, her brother-in-law persisted in keeping the feud alive. Her sons succumbed to their uncle's unholy influence and joined the feud, committed to seeking revenge for their father's death. Rita suffered to think her sons would be condemned to hell because of their actions and petitioned the Lord to take them before they committed any murders. Within a year, they both died of dysentery.

Free from familial obligations, Rita attempted to join the convent of St. Mary Magdalene in order to fulfill her lifelong desire to enter the religious life. Unfortunately, she was denied, ostensibly because the convent took only virgins and Rita was a widow. The nuns might have been avoiding scandal because she was the widow of a notorious man. Rita persisted, however, and they gave in to her petition on the condition that she complete an impossible task: she must attain peace between the feuding families. She immediately went to work on convincing the families to reconcile, and her success was rewarded with acceptance into the convent, where she remained until she died.

The Road to Forgiveness and Reconciliation

These three women demonstrate the power of prayer as a vehicle for hope. They each placed their trust in God, knowing his strength would see them through their struggles.

I was astonished to learn that my cousin Mertxe and Immaculée Ilibagiza were living across the lake from each other. One was suffering, and the other was working to alleviate part of the suffering. One had gone to offer hope; the other took hope, grew it into forgiveness, and then expanded it further to work toward reconciliation. Although it was essential, for their own sakes, for Rita and Immaculée to forgive the murderers of their loved ones, the next step they took, to seek reconciliation, truly opened their hearts to Christ. They worked to unify their communities and bring them back together as one, recognizing what God revealed to Immaculée: that all of them, *all of us*, are his beloved children.

questions to ponder

1. Define *peacemaker*. Name a woman in your life who fits your definition. How do her peacemaking efforts make her a figure of reconciliation?
2. Recall a time in your life when you were a peacemaker. What was the outcome? How did that make you feel?
3. Where in your spiritual life do you need reconciliation? Have you allowed yourself to fall into moments of despair? What does this chapter say to you about the source of hope?

Be a source of forgiveness and reconciliation to someone. Share how God has helped you find peace.

~~~~~~

authentic icons
of friendship
and community

Mother Antonia Brenner and St. Bibiana

~~~~~~

Friendship is born at that moment
when one man says to another:
"What! You too? I thought that no one but myself . . ."

~C. S. Lewis, *The Four Loves*

I ran across a fantastic piece of trivia: the patron saint of hang-overs is St. Bibiana. Yes, really. Of course, the very fact that I know this detail is in itself a little bit scandalous, since it naturally raises a related question: *Why would Maria need to know this?*

The truth is, several decades ago I might have needed recourse to St. Bibiana. Maybe just a little bit . . . when I was a bartender in a GI bar in West Germany.

In the months leading up to our wedding, while he was stationed in Bamberg, Germany, and I was still in the United States, John took on a number of odd jobs on the weekends to give us a little nest egg to start off our marriage. He worked at a local bar owned by a retired army warrant officer who hired soldiers on the weekends to handle things like stocking the coolers and working as bouncers. My big, strong husband made a fine bouncer. He deejayed, too, so he would alternate between those two jobs on the weekends.

After we got married and I joined him in Germany, John kept working at the bar every other weekend so we'd have plenty of play money. On the nights he worked, I'd sit at the bar and blow kisses to him in the deejay booth. One night, one of the bartenders didn't show up, and the owner asked me to fill in. The rest is history.

I became a pretty popular bartender. My bar usually brought in the most money, probably because I was a female. Okay, I'm pretty sure it was because I was the *only* female bartender. My husband didn't mind it since I was *behind* the bar—I drew the line at waiting tables on the crowded floor. The soldiers found out pretty quickly that my husband was the bouncer, so they behaved themselves for the most part, though I admit there was once a tiny little incident, and I might have actually thrown a punch in a brawl. Maybe.

A Friend in Need

When I arrived in Germany, my husband was the only person I knew. I was thousands of miles away from my family and friends.

The first couple of weeks were busy. John was still on leave, which gave us time to fill out paperwork and take care of important things like getting military ID cards and international driver's licenses. We would run errands in the morning, go sightseeing in the afternoon, and then have dinner in town;

we were learning to get around the installation and the city of Bamberg.

Eventually John's leave ran out; it was time for him to return to work and for me to figure out how to be a homemaker. Unfortunately, as soon as John went back to work he drew an assignment that sent him into the field for two weeks. I found myself alone, truly alone, for the first time in my life. I didn't quite know my way around town yet, and I didn't know anyone other than the bar patrons. They were fun, but not very deep conversationalists. It was also difficult to connect with people in the neighborhood; I didn't speak German, and I didn't encounter many who spoke English.

The first thing I did when John left was to get in the car and explore. I should have paid closer attention to his warnings about places that were off-limits to military dependents—I accidentally got on the autobahn headed to Berlin. In the years before the fall of the Berlin Wall and the reunification of Germany, American military personnel and their dependents were not allowed to venture into East Germany without a number of stamps and permissions. I was about to cause an international incident! And I didn't even know my street address. It scared me terribly, but in the rush of adrenaline I was able to find my way off the autobahn and back to our apartment, which I swore I wouldn't leave until John returned.

I felt as isolated as my mother must have felt when she first arrived in Atlanta, or my grandmother when she first arrived in Cuba. Several days into my lonely exile, at the peak of boredom that had driven me to clean the bathroom three days in a row, one of the women I'd met at the bar gave me a call to check up on me. Angelika was a German woman who lived close by and worked at a restaurant bar. Everyone in the local German restaurants always knew when a unit was in the field because business was slow, and she suspected that I was probably feeling lonely. How right she was!

I was about to clean the bathroom a fourth time when she called. For years, she would tease me about how quickly I accepted her invitation to go out for a beer. Looking back, I know with certainty that she was a godsend, truly sent by God to extend herself to me in friendship when I needed a friend so much. Angelika was my angel!

We bonded quickly over that beer, and it seemed as though we were best friends by the time John returned from the field. I think we were. The next year I was the matron of honor at her wedding. Although we now live thousands of miles apart, I think of her often and what a cherished friend she was to me. Her friendship, and what I learned about generosity in that first awkward exchange, has stayed with me and formed me in the subsequent friendships I've had as an adult.

Faithful Friendship

I have a dear friend who lives in another state, too far away to even imagine visiting with any kind of regularity, and yet somehow we manage to see each other several times a year. I think it's a miracle every time. She says it's our Mother, Mary, bringing her daughters together. I believe it.

This friend, too, has taught me a lot about true friendship. While I'm content to be in the same zip code with her, she goes out of her way to make me feel at home. She showers me with hospitality, from fresh flowers in the guest room to my favorite snacks. Perhaps most fun of all, she seems to be on a constant quest to surprise and amaze me with new things. I'm grateful for every big and little gift she gives me on these visits, but the greatest gift has been her magnanimous sharing of her faith with me. She has opened her heart to me and blessed me through her example, her gentle teachings, her deep love of the Lord. This treasured friendship has shown me the value of spiritual friendship, which demonstrates a practical truth: our earthly friendships teach us to become better friends to Jesus.

Several women have blessed me by offering such friendship out of nowhere, from outside my comfortable circle of friends. These beautiful women have entered my life and my heart to ease me out of the loneliness brought on by a move to another city or into a new stage of my life. They have shown up with an apple pie or a very nice bottle of wine and said, if not in words, then certainly in actions:

I want to be your friend. I see in you a kindred spirit.

I see in you a sister in Christ.

To be sure, this is one of the richest and most authentic forms of friendship, one based on a mutual understanding that our worth and our purpose comes from God and is for his glory. I haven't always had this kind of friendship in my life, and to have it now in such abundance is cause for celebration. So the wine flows—generously—at every opportunity I have to be with these cherished friends in faith.

I don't need to call upon St. Bibiana these days. Perhaps I've learned a bit of temperance. (Perhaps I'm just drinking better wine.)

Little is known about Bibiana except what is recorded in the martyrologies of the early Church. She lived and died in Rome at the time of Apronianus, governor in AD 363, who had an especially vindictive hatred of Christians. Her wealthy parents were murdered because of their devout Christian faith, and Bibiana, along with her sister, Demetria, was left to die in extreme poverty. Demetria succumbed to the harshness of their destitution, but Bibiana was ultimately tortured, tied to a pillar, and whipped to death.

A kindly priest took her body for burial, and over time, first a chapel and then a church were erected over her remains. Finally, sometime between 1624 and 1626, the church was rebuilt and Pope Urban VIII had her relics, and those of her parents and sister, secured there. Legends say that an herb that eases headaches grew around Bibiana's burial site, and somehow this associated her with the patronage of hangovers.

I've shared St. Bibiana's story with numerous friends as we've gathered to share an evening's glass of wine. I don't think her patronage was an intentionally comical one, but it does delight me, and it's a fun thing to share. Laughter always makes itself at home when I'm together with friends.

Our friends teach us about what's important and what isn't. Each of the women who have been close friends in various times in my life has taught me something about how to be a friend. Each time we gather together, whether in pairs or in larger gatherings, whether to share a burden or simply to pamper ourselves a bit, I come away enriched and refreshed. There is always something encouraging in the gathering of women friends.

In high school, I spent hours and hours on the phone with my very best friend; we talked forever about boys and dances and clothes. In retrospect, most of those conversations were about superficial things, but they were so important to us in the moment. As a young woman, I focused on the essentials: I needed support as a new wife and mother. Later I needed a different kind of support as a novice teacher. Getting together with groups of women friends was a joyful and sometimes cathartic experience that saw me through some difficult times.

I look back now on those days and see a void in spiritual support, and it saddens me. I didn't regret it at the time because I didn't know what I was missing, but now, of course, I know and seek that spiritual element of friendship, too. It has made all the difference in my midlife relationships, to enjoy deeper friendships that share friendship with Christ.

St. Bibiana, who drew me into her story because I thought her patronage was funny, has impressed me with the drawn out nature of her martyrdom. Bibiana wasn't killed immediately. Instead, she had everything taken from her. This trial must have been difficult for a young woman who had been well cared for by her parents. Poverty was cause for looking heavenward.

Bibiana models a very basic catechetical lesson: God made us to know him, love him, and serve him in this world, and to be happy with him in heaven. Whatever material losses she had, all the pain and suffering in the months leading to her torturous end were nothing compared to her salvation.

Bibiana knew and loved the Lord. His friendship was true and constant, giving her the strength and conviction to withstand her trials without wavering. While most modern women don't face the kinds of trials Bibiana endured, we do get caught up in the challenges of our modern world. Long work weeks and isolation can wear us down.

When I get together with my friends, we offer each other support and encouragement. Often, our gatherings serve as little pockets of relief from busy, scheduled lives in which we constantly put others ahead of ourselves. We take turns hosting our get-togethers, making an effort to set nice tables, provide delicious food, and pay attention to detail in order to delight each other and express our friendship. Our time together refreshes our spirits and renews our souls.

The Least of My Brothers and Sisters

Christ calls me to share with *everyone* all the essential qualities of friendship—service, unconditional love, attention—that I unselfishly share with *some* people. Some days I can do that better than others; it's clear to me that this is not an easy route to sainthood. It's easy for me to serve my loved ones because I believe they deserve my loving attention, and more. It's quite another thing to offer that friendship to strangers.

Our family supports the poor as well as prison ministries through our parish's St. Vincent de Paul Society. We started doing this work as a family one Christmas when our children were still young. The Angel Tree project to provide Christmas gifts for poor families needed Spanish-speaking volunteers, and we were recruited as a family to provide translations during the toy pickup.

We fell in love with the people we served and returned for many years. The program grew over time, adding the Angel Tree program for families whose primary breadwinners were imprisoned. I was moved by the gratitude expressed by the majority of the individuals we encountered; every once in a while, though, we'd encounter people who were less gracious. Anger fueled their attitudes and actions, and in truth they were difficult to love.

In my heart, I knew these people needed my love even more than the kind and grateful souls I met. And so I reminded myself, when faced with challenging cases, that these people carried burdens I could not see; I was not aware of their circumstances or why they were receiving aid from the prison ministry. It wasn't easy, but it was important.

This ministry required a higher level of emotional and spiritual risk than simply writing a check to feel I had fulfilled my duty to the poor and the marginalized. It was a level of risk I had not considered. Although I never felt I was in physical danger, ministering to these hurting people rocked my world, forcing me to examine the consequences of my beliefs. I had always said I was a Christian; I hadn't always understood what I was declaring.

A Real Prison Ministry

Some kindred spirits are easy to recognize even without meeting them in person. Mother Antonia Brenner has been a kind of spiritual mentor for me in that way, showing me through her life and legacy what it means to be willing to give everything—physically, financially, even relationally—to imitate the love of Christ in caring for the poor and downcast.

She was an unlikely candidate to choose this kind of sacrifice: a Beverly Hills socialite in the jet-setting 1950s and 1960s—a wife and mother accustomed to the comfort and the opulence of a mansion. Mother Antonia traded it all for an austere cell in a Mexican prison. By choice. She also founded a community of women who were too old (or otherwise "undesirable") to be welcomed into more traditional religious orders. The Eudist Servants of the Eleventh Hour is an organization for older, independent women who have chosen a life of service at "the eleventh hour"—toward the end of their lives, while they are still active and strong.

Most of the Servants serve the families of inmates still living in the prison in Tijuana, Mexico, where Mother Antonia lived in a ten-by-ten-foot prison cell with only a cot and a bible. She befriended the inmates and the guards, providing for their spiritual needs, but more than that, she loved them when they believed they were unlovable. Mother Antonia's audacity and courage to see the human soul through the eyes of Christ reminds me of that of Sr. Blandina Segale, who one hundred years earlier stood up to a lynch mob and dispersed it.

Prisons in the 1970s in Tijuana were dangerous places, but Mother Antonia was undaunted by the rough characters she encountered. She loved them all and trusted the Lord to take care of her. Once, a riot broke out in one of the prisons. All manner of violent acts played out, but Mother Antonia was determined to put an end to it immediately. She walked directly into the middle of the fray. The feuding factions immediately stood down, afraid she would be hurt in the fighting. What a woman! These hardened criminals softened at the sight of her. Mother Antonia radiated such love to these men that they had to put a stop to their hate.

She exemplified the often-used phrase "love the sinner, hate the sin." Her love and friendship extended beyond the bars of the prison to include the victims and the wardens as well, catechizing them all and no doubt bringing peace and reconciliation along the way. I don't know where she found her strength, but I like to think it came from seeing in each prisoner not the label of his crime, but his brotherhood to her through Christ.

Consoling Hearts

St. Bibiana died friendless. First she lost her parents and then her sister, Demetria. Imprisonment and death followed an imposed exile in which she must have been isolated from any friendly faces. Jesus was her only friend. At the other end of the spectrum is Mother Antonia Brenner, who left a life of comfort and community in order to seek out and befriend the friendless. Both women are signs of consolation for those who need a fresh vision of the consoling heart of Jesus.

What beautiful models of receiving and giving friendship! Imagine enduring the loneliness and isolation these women must have endured. St. Bibiana lost everything, and Mother Antonia Brenner gave it all up. I am encouraged by their example—to know and love Jesus so much that I can carry his love within me to my death or to those who most desperately need his Divine Friendship.

questions to ponder

1. Define *friendship*. Name a woman in your life who fits your definition. How does she exemplify friendship?

2. Recall a time in your life when you made a new friend. Did you initiate the relationship? How did that make you feel?

3. Do you have spiritual friendships? Do you have a friend or friends with whom you share your faith? Have you ever offered to pray with a friend?

Think of Jesus as your friend. Make a date to spend time with him in Adoration before the Blessed Sacrament.

~~~~~~

from badass to blessed

Virtuous Women Everywhere and the Blessed Virgin Mary

~~~~~~

Whatever is true, whatever is honorable, whatever is just, whatever is pure, whatever is pleasing, whatever is commendable, if there is any excellence and if there is anything worthy of praise, think about these things.

~Philippians 4:8

I first knew the Blessed Virgin Mary by the name my mother most often used for her when I was a little girl: *la virgencita.* Although the literal translation is "the little virgin," the Spanish diminutive connotes affection. There's nothing *little* about Mary, but she made herself small in the eyes of the world because of her humility.

La virgencita was small enough for a little girl to grasp Mary's goodness, joy, and love.

I learned more about Mary as I grew up, but that affectionate connection fostered by my mother has been a most important element in my relationship with the Blessed Mother. No matter what name I call her now, she's the same Mary. And she always answers.

Catholics have about a million names for Mary. They are all beautiful and all meaningful. I can use them all. However, a few of her titles are particular favorites of mine from different times in my life. I attended Catholic schools for most of my education, so I can list every school we played against in basketball: Our Lady of the Assumption; Immaculate Heart of Mary; Queen of Angels; and my personal favorite, Our Lady of Victory, whom we invoked before every game. My sister is devoted to Our Lady of Lourdes, so much so that she named her daughter after Our Lady. My oldest daughter, Victoria Maria, is named for Mary, too. I guess we can't help ourselves!

I have a friend devoted to Our Lady of Pilar and another devoted to Our Lady of the Snows. Yet another friend loves Our Lady of Guadalupe. I have three friends with devotions to Our Lady of Fatima. That title makes me smile because there's a small family restaurant in my town whose owner is Portuguese and named Fatima. Every time we go to dinner there, I count the number of kitschy plastic statues of Our Lady of Fatima scattered about the dining room. There's something about Fatima's devotion to Mary under this title that drives her customers to keep giving her more images of Our Lady. I hope that it pleases the Lord's mother.

I guess when we're talking about Our Mother, there's no such thing as too much affection. When my family goes on vacation to Hollywood, Florida, we attend a little church that has the most eclectic collection of statues of Our Lady I've ever seen. None of the statues match in style or color or even medium. If you love Mary, it's quite endearing. No doubt the statues were gifts from different immigrant parishioners who wanted to bring a little bit of their former homes to their new one.

Many of us, it seems to me, befriend Our Lady in some way that helps us define how we relate to her. Or maybe it's the other way around: maybe she helps us define who we are.

What's in a Name?

I was named after Mary, though I didn't always appreciate it. I was named after the Blessed Mother according to one of her lesser-known titles, Our Lady of Begoña. My first name is Maria, and my middle name is Begoña. My mom's name is Begoña, too, so that makes me Begoñita, "little Begoña." There's nothing diminutive about me, and anyway, I'm too old for that, so I go by Bego. It makes fielding phone calls at home a game of *"How do you know my mother?"* If the caller asks for any variation of Bego, my family members know it's a friend. If the request is for Maria, well . . . let's just say we have a pretty effective way of weeding out the telemarketers.

I'm named Begoña after my mother, of course, but there's a reason this particular name has significance in our family. Our Lady of Begoña is the patroness of the province of Biscay in the Basque country in northern Spain; her title derives from a region within Biscay. As my mother was the first child born in Cuba after her parents left Spain, the name connected Mom, and now me, to my grandparents' beloved homeland.

When I was a young woman I traveled one August to Bilbao, the capital of Biscay, and attended Mass at the Basilica of Begoña on the Feast of the Assumption of Mary, a special Marian feast, of course, but also one of two important festivals in Bilbao; the other is on October 11, which is the Feast of Our Lady of Begoña. I felt a call to schedule a pilgrimage there and pay a visit to *Amatxu*, an endearment for Our Lady in my grandparents' native Basque language that means "little mother."

In Cuba, Mary is known as *Cachita*, the diminutive of *Caridad* (Charity). And one day when I make another pilgrimage, this time to the National Shrine of Our Lady of Charity of El Cobre in Cuba, I know *Cachita* will receive me with open arms, as she always has.

So many names for Mary! And she answers to them all. But for me, the sweetest name for Our Mother is still *la virgencita*. It resonates with all the affection in my own mother's heart when she first spoke of the Blessed Mother to me. To use that name invokes all the feelings of love, security, and belonging I felt when I was in my mother's arms. All those names point to the same woman, and when she's sure she has our attention, she turns our gaze to her son, Jesus. To know Mary is to open ourselves to knowing Jesus.

May the Blessed Virgin Accompany You

There were many years in my life when I turned away from *la virgencita* and in the process also lost sight of her Son. I made a series of choices that added up; eventually, I found myself not attending Mass, no longer participating in the sacraments. I'm grateful that I saw my error, and grateful for the graces of the sacrament of Reconciliation. It has been a long reversion that started when my children were in sacrament preparation for First Holy Communion and continues through today. Every day I grow a little stronger in my faith.

As I reflect on my life, I can see things now that weren't apparent while I was experiencing them. I look at happy events in my life such as job changes or moving into a new house, or sad events such as the deaths of loved ones, and see where Mary's gentle hand was present. I turned away, but she didn't, and neither did Jesus. It was just as it is in a blessing my mother uses by way of saying good-bye: *Que la virgen te acompañe.* "May the Blessed Virgin accompany you."

I love the idea that Mary accompanies me, like a mother at a playground. She's present, keeping an eye on her children, sometimes calling to us to quit doing something wrong, ready to kiss a boo-boo, but mostly just watching over us as we play. This tender image of Mary, the Blessed Virgin, the Mother of God, Our Lady of Charity, our *Amatxu*, is a good place to begin, but she is so much more.

When I think of Mary, my first thought is of the story of the Nativity as described in Luke's Gospel. The second is the painting *Madonna and Child* by Giovanni Battista Salvi da Sassoferrato. The painting captures a tender moment between mother and child: the infant Jesus is sleeping, nestled in the warmth of Mary's neck, and she holds him close, resting her cheek upon his head. These images bring to mind Mary's maternity, her role as the mother of Jesus. I am awed by the immensity of the relationship. Who was this girl who became the Mother of God?

Although her life and role in salvation history are foretold in the Old Testament and documented in the New Testament, other aspects of her life are largely unknown or pieced together based on some historical documents and traditions of the time.

According to tradition, she was born to Saints. Joachim and Anne late in their lives, a blessing to them since they had prayed a long time to have a child. The doctrine of the Immaculate Conception holds that from the very moment of her conception, Mary was free from original sin, a singular grace reserved for her by God and imparted by the merits of her Son.

When she was a young woman, Mary received a message from an angel. He explained that she would bear a child, the Son of God the Father, through the Holy Spirit. Although Mary wondered how this could be since she had never known a man, she gave her assent and turned her life over entirely to God's will (see Lk 1:26–38).

Mary's exemplary obedience to God's will was no small thing. Her *yes* to God brought about the fulfillment of Isaiah's prophecy that a virgin would bear a son (see Is 7:14). Her willing participation in God's plan for salvation was an act of cooperation and obedience. Mary's *yes* was also a yes to cooperating in Christ's Passion and the redemption of the world. It's no wonder that from the moment of her Son's earthly existence she pondered all these things in her heart (see Lk 2:19).

Then she went to visit her cousin Elizabeth, who was also pregnant. What a joyful meeting! But it was more than that. Elizabeth's son, John the Baptist, leaped in his mother's womb as he sensed the presence of Jesus in Mary's womb. John was filled with the Holy Spirit, and that carried over to Elizabeth, who declared that Mary was the mother of her Lord (see Lk 1:39–44). Mary's suffering must have started soon thereafter. Although she was betrothed to Joseph, they weren't married yet, and it was inevitable that he would learn she was pregnant. Joseph rejected her, presuming she had been with another man. Perhaps wanting to avoid scandal, he discreetly made plans to divorce Mary. However, an angel of the Lord came to Joseph in a dream and eased Joseph's misgivings. Joseph brought Mary into his home and together they prepared for Jesus's birth (see Mt 1:18–25).

At about this time, Emperor Augustus declared a census, and Joseph was required to report to Bethlehem (see Lk 2:1–6). He traveled there with Mary, who was due to give birth soon. When Jesus was born, they laid him in a manger—he came into the world not as a king with finery and pomp, but rather in the humblest of circumstances.

When Mary and Joseph presented Jesus at the temple in accordance with religious law and custom, Mary received a prophecy from the elderly Simeon, a pious, prayerful man who recognized Jesus as the Messiah. He told Mary that one day Jesus would be misunderstood and opposed and that she would suffer with him—a sword would pierce her heart. We know nothing of what Mary might have suffered with this knowledge, since she kept all these things within her heart (see Lk 2:22–35).

The tender imagery of the Sassoferrato Madonna drives home to me what those first years must have been like for Mary, holding the child Jesus close to her heart. How affectionately she must have held him! These early events in Mary's life describe her beautiful maternal side; in addition to being Jesus Christ's mother, Mary is also the mother of the Church. She is our spiritual mother because we are part of the Body of Christ. We receive, just as Jesus did, her love, nurture, and care . . . but also her instruction in the virtues and tenets of the faith, for we know that Mary was a pious woman.

Her gentle guidance always points us to Jesus.

An Ongoing Relationship with the Blessed Virgin

Mary's story doesn't end with the birth of Jesus. Her role in the Incarnation of Our Lord is, of course, what we know best, but her story expands from that point on. She was present at Jesus's first miracle at the wedding in Cana. She was present at the Crucifixion. She was present when the Church was founded at Pentecost. Mary is our intercessor, spiritual mother, and model of complete submission to the holy will of God.

Mary was the first and perfect disciple; I look to her to show me my role in the New Evangelization. Mary brought Jesus into the world through his birth. I can bring Jesus to the world—I do it every day as circumstances in my life allow.

I am like Mary in my home. I am a dedicated wife to my husband, as Mary was to her earthly spouse, St. Joseph. I am a mother to three children whom I nurtured, cared for, instructed, and taught the faith. I am a spiritual mother to two godchildren whom I love as dearly as I do my own children. In the workplace, I endeavor to model a Christian attitude. On the Internet, through my work in podcasting, blogging, and social media, I endeavor to spread the Good News by providing relevant content as well as maintaining a presence that leads others to Christ.

God had a plan for Mary, and she accepted it. Her *fiat*, her commitment to "let it be done," was given freely; she lived her life on earth in cooperation with God's will. Like Mary, I am committed to being the person God created me to be.

We can and should develop a relationship with Mary that will continue to blossom throughout our lives. Devotions such as the Rosary or chaplets can enrich our prayer lives. A more serious commitment, such as a consecration to Jesus through Mary, is an intentional way to give oneself to Jesus. Mary is present in all these devotions and is leading us to her Son.

Mary, Queen of All Saints

Mary's title of Queen of All Saints inspires me to live the life God meant for me by seeking the holy example of the saints. The faithful women whose lives I explored in the previous chapters are just a sampling of the amazing women we find in the Communion of Saints, the common-union of the Body of Christ of which we're all a part, whether on earth or in heaven.

My goal, of course, is to get to heaven, and the women in these pages demonstrate virtues or special qualities that illuminate a path for me to follow. I wrote at the beginning of this book that I wanted to surround myself with extraordinary women in order to emulate them. As I journeyed with these women, I found that each one taught me something of being a woman of

God, demonstrating a particular virtue that leads to goodness. These women brought me little pieces of Mary as I prayed with them; together, they moved me toward Mary, who is the embodiment of all the virtues.

One of my favorite prayers is the Litany of the Saints, the longest version possible. I love to recite it and especially to chant it. It's all beautiful to me. Now, I pray an abbreviated litany:

St. Teresa of Avila, model of audacity, pray for us.

St. Joan of Arc, model of courage, pray for us.

St. Helena of Constantinople, model of a missionary heart, pray for us.

St. Catherine of Siena, model of advocacy, pray for us.

St. Gianna Beretta Molla, model of human dignity, pray for us.

St. Christina the Astonishing, model of selflessness, pray for us.

St. Margaret of Antioch, model of perseverance, pray for us.

St. Rose of Lima, model of true beauty, pray for us.

Bl. Rosalie Rendu, model of compassion, pray for us.

St. Rita of Cascia, model of peacemaking, pray for us.

St. Bibiana, model of friendship, pray for us.

Our Lady of Charity, model of love, pray for us.

Blessed Mother, Queen of All Saints, pray for us.

Lord, have mercy on us.

Each of these saints lived a virtuous life, but Mary, Our Mother, excelled in *every* virtue. It isn't just that she surpasses the other saints in holiness, but that as the vessel of the grace given to her by God, she uses every bit of that grace and *magnifies* it. This becomes especially evident to me when I pray the Rosary, one of my favorite devotions. I give my petitions to Mary, confident that she'll intercede for me and confident still more that putting the graces and benefits of my prayer into her hands will magnify them for those who most need them.

I look to Mary as a reminder that God calls us to a life of holiness on earth so that we can become saints in heaven. I look to Mary as a model for this holiness, and I pray for the grace to achieve it in order to live in God's presence eternally.

Mary teaches us, by the example of her *yes* to God, how to live the greatest commandment of the Law:

> "Love the Lord your God with all your heart, and with all your soul, and with all your mind." This is the greatest and first commandment. And a second is like it: "Love your neighbor as yourself." (Mt 22:37–39)

Mary wants this for us, her children—that we love her Son and love each other. The women in these pages rose to the occasions in which they found themselves, performing heroic deeds for the love of God and the love of neighbor. We call them heroines. Many of them were holy women. But holiness does not come from doing heroic deeds; rather, holiness comes from doing God's will perfectly. That's heroic. That's badass. And that's the example I want to follow.

Que la virgen te acompañe.

questions to ponder

1. How would you describe your relationship with the Blessed Virgin Mary? Does she seem remote and enigmatic, a solemn figure who gazes down at you at Mass? Do you look to her for inspiration? Do you ask for her powerful intercession?

2. What has Mary taught you about being a woman? A mother or spiritual mother? A holy spouse? A disciple of Christ? What have you noticed about her in Scripture?

3. How might Mary be a spiritual companion for you?

Ask Mary to show herself to you as your spiritual mother, and invite her to help you grow in virtue.

I always thought writing a book was a solitary act: a taxing, emotionally exhausting, repetitive, hard, and often lonely endeavor. Boy was I wrong. Although there were many times I had to be alone, to put words on the page or edit, it wasn't a solitary act, and I was rarely lonely.

It did take a lot of hard work, much of it from other people. I'd like to thank all the good people at Ave Maria Press, including my editor, Heidi Saxton, who reached out to me to send her a proposal for a wild idea because she believed I could do it, and copyeditor Christina Nichols, whose gift of moving a word here or there made me a better writer. In fact, to the whole editorial team at Ave, who talked me off a ledge and convinced me to embrace my badass project, *even with the name*: thanks from the bottom of my heart.

To the original crew at Ink'n Doodle, Rob Suarez, Chuch Areces, Wency Ortega, and Achi Tuñón—go create something!

Thanks to Greg Willits, who first introduced me to blogging at Rosary Army and then invited me to collaborate on *That Catholic Show*; and Jennifer Willits, who would say all the words I put in her mouth: I love you guys!

Hugs and shenanigans to my pals at *Catholic Weekend*: Captain Jeff Nielsen, Steve Nelson, Fr. Cory Sticha, and Sarah Vabulas. Thanks for the prayers, encouragement, and support.

A million thanks to my favorite diva, Lisa Hendey—founder of *CatholicMom.com*, amazing author, kind editor, but most of all, dear friend—for your encouragement and support.

A most heartfelt thanks to my writing buddy, prayer warrior, shenanigans partner, and sister in Christ, Pat Gohn, for a lovely foreword, a memorable toast, and the gift of spiritual friendship that put a pen back in my hand.

To all my pals, near and far, who keep asking when the book will be ready: Here it is! Thanks, Linda, Jill, Leonie, Mary, Karen, Kristen, Yuyi, Ani, Isa; all of you!

To my family—brothers and sisters, nieces and nephews, tías and tíos—thanks for believing in me and sharing in my joy!

To my beloved children, Vicky, Christy, and Jonathan. You guys are the apple of my eye. Remember you have a streak of badassery in you.

And to my husband, John—my best friend, chief instigator, and hand-holder—thanks for dreaming with me.

my badass book of saints

six-week study guide

Week One: Introduction and Chapters One and Two

This week we'll be discussing the audacious Sr. Blandina Segale and St. Teresa of Ávila and the courageous Nancy Wake and St. Joan of Arc.

Opening

1. Discuss the title of the book. Do you find it shocking, or does a part of you smirk a little and wonder about the content? How do you think this book will compare to other books on the saints you've already read?

2. What does the author say about her choice to use the word *badass*?

3. The author uses the Spanish word *tremenda*. Define it. Are you *tremenda*?

Sharing

1. Offer your definitions of *audacity* and *courage*.

2. Discuss real women you know who have these qualities. How do they exemplify these qualities in their lives?

3. How about you? Do you have these qualities or wish you did?

4. Share a moment in your life when you demonstrated audacity or courage.

Inquiry

1. Do you know any other stories from the lives of St. Teresa of Ávila and St. Joan of Arc? Identify events in their lives that

demonstrate audacity or courage. How were they received by their peers or community? Their superiors?

2. In what ways were these women similar? How were they different?

3. What do they have in common with the women you know? What do they have in common with you?

Application

- Commit an act of audacity in your spiritual life.

    Discuss ways to integrate something new and daring into your faith journey. Is there a class you've wanted to take? Do you feel called to *teach* a class? Is there a ministry in your parish you'd like to try? Maybe you'd like to join a Bible study. Stretch yourself!

- Take one courageous step in response to Christ's call.

    Have you been away from the sacraments and do you want to return? Do you desire to make a deeper commitment to the Lord?

Week Two: Chapters Three and Four

This week we'll be discussing adventurers Edel Quinn and St. Helena and the eloquent Mother Mary Lange and St. Catherine of Siena.

Sharing

1. Offer your definitions of *missionary* and *advocacy*.

2. Discuss real women you know who have these qualities. How do they exemplify these qualities in their lives?

3. How about you? Do you have these qualities or wish you did?

4. Share a moment in your life when you demonstrated a missionary heart or spoke truth to those in power.

Inquiry

1. Do you know any other stories from the lives of St. Helena and St. Catherine of Siena? Identify events in their lives when they demonstrated a missionary heart or spoke truth

to those in power. How were they received by their peers or community? Their superiors?

2. In what ways were these women similar? How were they different?

3. What do they have in common with the women you know? What do they have in common with you?

Application

- Be a shining light of Christ's love to others as you go about your day.

  What part of your spiritual life do you want to share with others? Do you enjoy leading group prayer such as a Rosary or chaplet? Do you have a special skill or love of a devotion that you would like to share with others?

- Speak the truth. Be an advocate for positive change.

  Do you recognize an individual or group in your community in need of a voice? Is there a situation that needs to be addressed lovingly?

Week Three: Chapters Five and Six

This week we'll be discussing the valiant Phyllis Bowman and St. Gianna Beretta Molla and the selfless Irena Sendler and St. Christina the Astonishing.

Sharing

1. Offer your definitions of *respect for human dignity* and *selflessness*.

2. Discuss real women you know who have these qualities. How do they exemplify these qualities in their lives?

3. How about you? Do you have these qualities or wish you did?

4. Share a moment in your life when you demonstrated respect for human dignity or selflessness.

Inquiry

1. Do you know any other stories from the lives of St. Gianna Beretta Molla and St. Christina the Astonishing? Identify events in their lives that demonstrate respect for human

dignity or selflessness. How were they received by their peers or community? Their superiors?

2. In what ways were these women similar? How were they different?
3. What do they have in common with the women you know? What do they have in common with you?

Application

*   Seek moments in your interactions with others to make eye contact and acknowledge their worth.

    What are some ways you can serve others with dignity?

*   Think of something that needs to be done that no one else is handling. Be the hands and feet of Christ this week.

    Is there a place in your spiritual life that demands that you die to self? Is there a ministry or other need that would benefit from your sacrifice of time or talent?

Week Four: Chapters Seven and Eight

This week we'll be discussing the eloquent Flannery O'Connor and St. Margaret of Antioch and the beautiful Audrey Hepburn and St. Rose of Lima.

Sharing

1. Offer your definitions of *perseverance* and *beauty*.
2. Discuss real women you know who have these qualities. How do they exemplify these qualities in their lives?
3. How about you? Do you have these qualities or wish you did?
4. Share a moment in your life when you demonstrated perseverance or shared your inner beauty.

Inquiry

1. Do you know any other stories from the lives of St. Margaret of Antioch and St. Rose of Lima? Identify events in their lives that demonstrate perseverance or inner beauty. How were they received by their peers or community? Their superiors?

2. In what ways were these women similar? How were they different?
3. What do they have in common with the women you know? What do they have in common with you?

Application

- Ask a saint to pray for you as you persevere through your trials.

   Where in your spiritual life do you need perseverance? Have you taken on a new devotion or discipline? Are you struggling with making a change?

- Thank Jesus for those qualities that make you beautiful. Offer them to the Blessed Virgin Mary and ask her to magnify them in you in the service of her Son.

   What makes you beautiful? List those qualities. Embrace them. How can your inner beauty inspire others? Do you serve with a smile? Do you love others, even when it is difficult?

Week Five: Chapters Nine and Ten

This week we'll be discussing the compassionate Dorothea Lange and Bl. Rosalie Rendu and the resolute Immaculée Ilibagiza and St. Rita of Cascia.

Sharing

1. Offer your definitions of *compassion* and *peacemaker*.
2. Discuss real women you know who have these qualities. How do they exemplify these qualities in their lives?
3. How about you? Do you have these qualities or wish you did?
4. Share a moment in your life when you demonstrated compassion or peacemaking.

Inquiry

1. Do you know any other stories from the lives of Bl. Rosalie Rendu and St. Rita of Cascia? Identify events in their lives

that demonstrate compassion or peacemaking. How were they received by their peers or community? Their superiors?

2. In what ways were these women similar? How were they different?

3. What do they have in common with the women you know? What do they have in common with you?

Application

• Listen to someone with your heart. Don't say anything or offer advice. Just listen and be present.

   Where in your spiritual life do you need compassion? Have you ever considered spending a morning working in a soup kitchen or making sandwiches for distribution? Do you ever visit the poor or sick?

• Be a source of forgiveness and reconciliation to someone. Share how God has helped you find peace.

   Where in your spiritual life do you need reconciliation? Have you allowed yourself to fall into moments of despair?

Week Six: Chapter Eleven and the Conclusion

This week we'll be discussing the authentic Mother Antonia Brenner and St. Bibiana and our model of virtue, the Blessed Virgin Mary.

Sharing

1. Offer your definitions of *friendship* and *virtue*.

2. Discuss real women you know who have these qualities. How do they exemplify these qualities in their lives?

3. How about you? Do you have these qualities or wish you did?

4. Share a moment in your life when you demonstrated friendship or sought to grow in virtue.

Inquiry

1. What is your favorite image, expression, or story about Jesus's mother, the Blessed Virgin Mary?

2. What struck you about the story of Mother Antonia Brenner, in how she imitated Mary? Identify events in the lives of both women that demonstrate friendship or virtue. How were they received by their peers or community? Their superiors?
3. What does the story of St. Bibiana say to us about the gift and necessity of friendship?
4. In what ways are these women similar? How were they different? What do they have in common with the women you know? What do they have in common with you?

Application

- Think of Jesus as your friend. Make a date to spend time with him in Adoration before the Blessed Sacrament.

    Do you have spiritual friendships? Do you have a friend or friends with whom you share your faith? Have you ever offered to pray with a friend?

- Ask Mary to show herself to you as your spiritual mother, and invite her to help you grow in virtue.

    How would you describe your relationship with the Blessed Virgin Mary? Do you look to her for inspiration? Do you ask for her powerful intercession?

    What has Mary taught you about being a woman? A mother or spiritual mother? A holy spouse? A disciple of Christ?

    How might Mary be a spiritual companion for you?

Closing

1. What did you learn or take away from the book?
2. Who are the women or saints with whom you identified the most?
3. How has the book affected you? Do you have a desire to learn more about the saints? Are you inspired to own your badass qualities as a Christian woman?

4. Make a list of the saints who inspire you. Create your own small litany. Ask those saints to be powerful intercessors for you.

Introduction: From Badass to Blessed

"Our Lady of Begoña." St. Mary Star of the Sea. http://www.stmaryswest
melbourne.org/wp/content/uploads/2013/09/
Begona0.pdf.

"Our Lady of Begoña." *Wikipedia*. Last modified October 3, 2014. http://
en.wikipedia.org/wiki/Our_Lady_of_Begoña.

1. Audacious Sisters Who Acted Fearlessly

Archdiocese of Santa Fe. "Archbishop Michael J. Sheehan to Hold Joint
Press Conference with CHI St. Joseph's Children to Announce Vatican's
Immediate Permission to Open the Sainthood Cause of Servant of God,
Sister Blandina Segale, SC." Press release. June 25, 2014. http://www.
archdiocesesantafe.org/Offices/Communications/PressReleases/
14.0624PressConfOfficial.pdf.

Contreras, Russell. "'Fastest Nun in the West': Blandina Segale on Path for
Sainthood." June 25, 2014. *The Huffington Post*. http://www.huffington
post.com/2014/06/25/fastest-nun-in-the-west_n_5531926.html.

Segale, Blandina. *At the End of the Santa Fe Trail*. Milwaukee, WI: Bruce Publishing Company, 1948.

St. Teresa of Avila. *Autobiography of St. Teresa of Avila*. New York: Dover Pub-
lications, Inc., 2010.

"St. Teresa of Avila." New Advent. http://www.newadvent.org/
cathen/14515b.htm.

"St. Teresa of Avila." EWTN. http://www.ewtn.com/library/MARY/Avila.
htm.

2. Courageous Soldiers Who Fought Real, Meaningful Battles

"Nancy Wake." Badass of the Week. April 26, 2013. http://
badassoftheweek.com/index.cgi?id=27450552861.

"St. Joan of Arc." EWTN. http://www.ewtn.com/library/MARY/JOAN
.htm.

"St. Joan of Arc." New Advent. http://www.newadvent.orgcathen/08409c.
htm.

Ward, Paul Stanley. "Nancy Wake: The White Mouse." *NZEDGE.com*, April
19, 2000. http://www.nzedge.com/nancy-wake/.

3. Missionary Adventurers Who Had a Heart for the World

O'Regan, Mary. "Ten Catholic Women Who Changed the World."
    Catholic Herald. May 31, 2012. http://www.catholicherald.co.uk/
    features/2012/05/31/ten-catholic-women-who-changed-the-world/.

"St. Helena." New Advent. http://www.newadvent.org/cathen/
    07202b.htm.

"Venerable Edel Mary Quinn." CatholicSaints.Info. http://catholicsaints.
    info/venerable-edel-mary-quinn/.

"Venerable Edel Quinn." Legion of Mary. http://www.legionofmary.ie/
    causes/profile/edel-quinn.

4. Outspoken Advocates Who Challenged the Status Quo

"The Cause of Canonization: Mother Mary Lange." The Mother Mary Lange
    Guild. http://www.motherlange.org/history.html.

"Elizabeth Clarisse Lange." The National Black Catholic Conference.
    http://nbccongress.org/black-catholics/elizabeth-clarisse-lange-fa-
    mous-blacks.asp.

"Mother Mary Lange." Oblate Sisters of Providence. http://www.oblatesist
    ers.com/MotherLange.html.

"St. Catherine of Siena." New Advent. http://www.newadvent.org/
    cathen/03447a.htm.

5. Valiant Women Who Lived and Died to Uphold Human Dignity

Andrusko, Dave. "Phyllis Bowman, RIP." *National Right to Life News Today*.
    May 8, 2012. http://www.nationalrighttolifenews.org/news/2012/05/
    phyllis-bowman-rip/#.VZafqvlViko.

"Homily of John Paul II: Santa Clara, Cuba, Thursday 22 January 1998."
    Vatican.va. http://w2.vatican.va/content/john-paul-ii/en/homi
    lies/1998/documents/hf_jp-ii_hom_19980122_santa-clara.html.

"Saint Gianna Beretta Molla: Wife, Mother, Doctor, Prolife Witness." The
    Society of Saint Gianna Beretta Molla. http://saintgianna.org/main.
    htm.

6. Selfless Saviors Who Did What Needed to Be Done

"Homily of John Paul II: Santa Clara, Cuba, Thursday 22 January 1998."
    Vatican.va. http://w2.vatican.va/content/john-paul-ii/en/homi
    lies/1998/documents/hf_jp-ii_hom_19980122_santa-clara.html.

"Irena Sendler." *Jewish Virtual Library*. https://www.jewishvirtuallibrary.
    org/jsource/biography/irenasendler.html.

"Life in a Jar: The Irena Sendler Project." http://www.irenasendler.org/.

"St. Christina the Astonishing." Catholic Exchange. December 15, 2014.
    http://catholicexchange.com/st-christina-the-astonishing.

7. Eloquent Images of Perseverance and Strength

Gordon, Sarah. "Flannery O'Connor (1925–1964)." *New Georgia Encyclopedia.* July 10, 2002. http://www.georgiaencyclopedia.org/articles/arts-culture/flannery-oconnor-1925-1964.

O'Connor, Flannery. *The Habit of Being: Letters of Flannery O'Connor.* Selected and edited by Sally Fitzgerald. New York: Farrar, Straus, Giroux, 1979.

O'Connor, Flannery. *Mystery and Manners: Occasional Prose.* New York: Farrar, Straus, Giroux, 1969.

"St. Margaret of Antioch." Catholic Online. http://www.catholic.org/saints/saint.php?saint_id=199.

8. Passionate Beauties Who Made the World a Better Place

"Audrey Hepburn Quotes." Biography Online. https://www.biographyonline.net/humanitarian/hepburn-quotes.html.

"Audrey Hepburn." *Wikipedia.* Last modified July 2, 2015. http://en.wikipedia.org/wiki/Audrey_Hepburn.

Paris, Barry. *Audrey Hepburn.* New York: Putnam, 1996.

"St. Rose of Lima." Catholic Online. http://www.catholic.org/saints/saint.php?saint_id=446.

9. Compassionate Souls Who Helped the Hopeless and Suffering

"Dorothea Lange: Biography." Biography.com. http://www.biography.com/people/dorothea-lange-9372993#early-years.

Gordon, Linda. *Dorothea Lange: A Life Beyond Limits.* London: W. W. Norton & Company, 2010.

"Homily of John Paul II: Feast of the Dedication of the Lateran Basilica, Sunday, 9 November 2003." Libreria Editrice Vaticana. http://w2.vatican.va/content/john-paul-ii/en/homilies/2003/documents/hf_jp-ii_hom_20031109_beatifications.html.

"Rosalie Rendu (1786–1856)." Vatican.va. http://www.vatican.va/news_services/liturgy/saints/ns_lit_doc_20031109_rendu_en.html.

10. Resolute Seekers of Peace and Reconciliation

Ilibagiza, Immaculée, and Steve Erwin. *Left to Tell: Discovering God Amidst the Rwandan Holocaust.* Carlsbad, CA: Hay House, 2006.

"Immaculée." www.immaculee.com.

"Life of Saint Rita." National Shrine of Saint Rita of Cascia. http://www.saintritashrine.org/life-of-saint-rita/.

11. Authentic Icons of Friendship and Community

Jordan, Mary, and Kevin Sullivan. *The Prison Angel: Mother Antonia's Journey from Beverly Hills to a Life of Service in a Mexican Jail.* New York: Penguin, 2005.

"St. Bibiana." Catholic Exchange. December 2, 2014. http://catholicexchange.com/st-bibiana-viviana.

Yardley, William. "Antonia Brenner, 'Prison Angel' Who Took Inmates Under Her Wing, Is Dead at 86." *The New York Times*. http://www.nytimes.com/2013/10/21/us/antonia-brenner-prison-angel-who-took-inmates-under-her-wings-dies-at-86.html?_r=0.

Conclusion: From Badass to Blessed

Hendey, Lisa M. *A Book of Saints for Catholic Moms: 52 Companions for Your Heart, Mind, Body, and Soul*. Notre Dame, IN: Ave Maria Press, 2011.

"Our Lady of Charity." *Wikipedia*. Last modified June 14, 2015. http://en.wikipedia.org/wiki/Our_Lady_of_Charity.

Sri, Edward. *Walking with Mary: A Biblical Journey from Nazareth to the Cross*. New York: Image, 2013.

Maria Morera Johnson is a *CatholicMom.com* blogger and cohost of SPQN's *Catholic Weekend*. She is a composition and literature professor and director of English learning support at Georgia Piedmont Technical College, working with nontraditional students in innovative success initiatives. She has received a number of awards for teaching.

She speaks on behalf of and consults with several organizations, including St. Vincent de Paul (Vincentians). Johnson helped organize the Catholic New Media Conference. Johnson often presents at national education conferences to encourage women in nontraditional fields to pursue their educational goals.

Johnson is a native of Cuba. Her first book, *Confessions of a Middle-Aged Cubanita*, was self-published. She and her husband, John, have three grown children and live in Conyers, Georgia.

AVE

AVE MARIA PRESS

Founded in 1865, Ave Maria Press,
a ministry of the Congregation of
Holy Cross, is a Catholic publishing
company that serves the spiritual and
formative needs of the Church and its
schools, institutions, and ministers;
Christian individuals and families; and
others seeking spiritual nourishment.

For a complete listing of titles from

Ave Maria Press

Sorin Books

Forest of Peace

Christian Classics

visit www.avemariapress.com

AVE MARIA PRESS
Notre Dame, IN
A Ministry of the United States Province of Holy Cross